The AWK
Programming
Language

The AWK
Programming
Language

ALFRED V. AHO
BRIAN W. KERNIGHAN
PETER J. WEINBERGER

AT&T Bell Laboratories
Murray Hill, New Jersey

ADDISON-WESLEY PUBLISHING COMPANY
Reading, Massachusetts • Menlo Park, California • New York
Don Mills, Ontario • Wokingham, England • Amsterdam • Bonn
Sydney • Singapore • Tokyo • Madrid • Bogotá
Santiago • San Juan

This book is in the **Addison-Wesley Series in Computer Science**

Michael A. Harrison
Consulting Editor

Library of Congress Cataloging-in-Publication Data
Aho, Alfred V.
    The AWK programming language.
    Includes index.
    1. AWK (Computer program language)   I. Kernighan,
Brian W.   II. Weinberger, Peter J.   III. Title.
QA76.73.A95A35   1988   005.13'3   87-17566
ISBN 0-201-07981-X

This book was typeset in Times Roman and Courier by the authors, using an Autologic APS-5 phototypesetter and a DEC VAX 8550 running the 9th Edition of the UNIX® operating system.

Reprinted with corrections October, 1988

AT&T

18 19 20-CRS-97 96 95 94

PREFACE

Computer users spend a lot of time doing simple, mechanical data manipulation — changing the format of data, checking its validity, finding items with some property, adding up numbers, printing reports, and the like. All of these jobs ought to be mechanized, but it's a real nuisance to have to write a special-purpose program in a standard language like C or Pascal each time such a task comes up.

Awk is a programming language that makes it possible to handle such tasks with very short programs, often only one or two lines long. An awk program is a sequence of patterns and actions that tell what to look for in the input data and what to do when it's found. Awk searches a set of files for lines matched by any of the patterns; when a matching line is found, the corresponding action is performed. A pattern can select lines by combinations of regular expressions and comparison operations on strings, numbers, fields, variables, and array elements. Actions may perform arbitrary processing on selected lines; the action language looks like C but there are no declarations, and strings and numbers are built-in data types.

Awk scans the input files and splits each input line into fields automatically. Because so many things are automatic — input, field splitting, storage management, initialization — awk programs are usually much smaller than they would be in a more conventional language. Thus one common use of awk is for the kind of data manipulation suggested above. Programs, a line or two long, are composed at the keyboard, run once, then discarded. In effect, awk is a general-purpose programmable tool that can replace a host of specialized tools or programs.

The same brevity of expression and convenience of operations make awk valuable for prototyping larger programs. One starts with a few lines, then refines the program until it does the desired job, experimenting with designs by trying alternatives quickly. Since programs are short, it's easy to get started, and easy to start over when experience suggests a different direction. And it's straightforward to translate an awk program into another language once the design is right.

Organization of the Book

The first goal of this book is to teach you what awk is and how to use it effectively. Chapter 1 is a tutorial on the bare minimum necessary to get started; after reading even a few pages, you should have enough information to begin writing useful programs. The examples in this chapter are very short and simple, typical of the interactive use of awk.

Chapter 2 covers the entire language in a systematic order. Although there are plenty of examples in this chapter, like most manuals it's long and a bit dry, so you will probably want to skim it on a first reading.

The rest of the book contains a wide variety of examples, chosen to show the breadth of applicability of awk and how to make good use of its facilities. Some of the programs are in regular use in our environment; others show ideas but are not intended for production use; a few are included just because they are fun.

The emphasis in Chapter 3 is on retrieval, transformation, reduction and validation of data — the tasks that awk was originally designed for. There is also a discussion of how to handle data like address lists that naturally comes in multiline chunks.

Awk is a good language for managing small, personal databases. Chapter 4 discusses the generation of reports from databases, and builds a simple relational database system and query language for data stored in multiple files.

Awk handles text with much the same convenience that most languages handle numbers, so it often finds application in text processing. Chapter 5 describes programs for generating text, and some that help with document preparation. One of the examples is an indexing program based on the one we used for this book.

Chapter 6 is about "little languages," that is, specialized languages that focus on a narrow domain. Awk is convenient for writing small translators because its basic operations support many of the lexical and table-management tasks encountered in translation. The chapter includes an assembler, a graphics language, and several calculators.

Awk is a good language for expressing certain kinds of algorithms. Because there are no declarations and because storage management is easy, an awk program has many of the advantages of pseudo-code but awk programs can be run, which is not true of pseudo-code. The focus in Chapter 7 is on experimentation with algorithms, including testing and performance evaluation. It shows several sorting algorithms, and culminates in a version of the Unix make program.

Chapter 8 describes some of the historical reasons why awk is as it is, and offers some suggestions on what to do when it is too slow or too confining.

Appendix A is a summary of the language; Appendix B contains answers to selected exercises.

You should begin by reading Chapter 1, and trying some small examples of your own. Go through Chapter 2 quickly, concentrating on the summaries and tables; don't get bogged down in the details. Then read as far into each of the subsequent chapters as your interest takes you. The chapters are nearly independent of each other, so the order doesn't matter much.

The Examples

There are several themes in the examples. The primary one, of course, is to show how to use awk well. We have tried to include a wide variety of useful constructions, and we have stressed particular aspects like associative arrays and regular expressions that typify awk programming.

A second theme is to show awk's versatility. Awk programs have been used from databases to circuit design, from numerical analysis to graphics, from compilers to system administration, from a first language for nonprogrammers to the implementation language for software engineering courses. We hope that the diversity of applications illustrated in the book will suggest new possibilities to you as well.

A third theme is to show how common computing operations are done. The book contains a relational database system, an assembler and interpreter for a toy computer, a graph-drawing language, a recursive-descent parser for an awk subset, a file-update program based on make, and many other examples. In each case, a short awk program conveys the essence of how something works in a form that you can understand and play with.

We have also tried to illustrate a spectrum of ways to attack programming problems. Rapid prototyping is an approach that awk supports well. A less obvious strategy is divide and conquer: breaking a big job into small components, each concentrating on one aspect of the problem. Another is writing programs that create other programs. Little languages define a good user interface and often suggest a sound implementation. Although these ideas are presented here in the context of awk, they are much more generally applicable, and ought to be part of every programmer's repertoire.

The examples have all been tested directly from the text, which is in machine-readable form. We have tried to make the programs error-free, but we have not added features nor made them proof against all possible invalid inputs, preferring to concentrate on conveying the essentials.

Evolution of the AWK Language

Awk was originally designed and implemented by the authors in 1977, in part as an experiment to see how the Unix tools grep and sed could be generalized to deal with numbers as well as text. It was based on our interests in regular expressions and programmable editors. Although it was meant for writing very short programs, its combination of facilities soon attracted users who wrote significantly larger programs. These larger programs needed features that had not been part of the original implementation, so awk was enhanced in a new version made available in 1985.

The major new feature is the ability for users to define their own functions.

Other enhancements include dynamic regular expressions, with text substitution and pattern-matching functions; additional built-in functions and variables; some new operators and statements; input from multiple files; and access to command-line arguments. Error messages have also been improved. The examples in Chapter 1 use only facilities of the original version; many examples in later chapters take advantage of new features.

This version of awk is part of Unix System V Release 3.1. Source code for this version is also available through AT&T's Unix System Toolchest software distribution system; call 1-201-522-6900 and log in as guest. In Europe, contact AT&T Unix Europe in London (44-1-567-7711); in the Far East, contact AT&T Unix Pacific in Tokyo (81-3-431-3670).

Since awk was developed under Unix, some of its features reflect capabilities usually found only there; these features are used in some of our examples. Furthermore, we have assumed the existence of some Unix utilities, particularly sort, for which exact equivalents may not exist elsewhere. Aside from these limitations, however, awk should be useful in any environment; in particular, it runs on MS-DOS. Further information is available from Addison-Wesley.

Awk is certainly not perfect; it has its share of irregularities, omissions, and just plain bad ideas, and it's sometimes painfully slow. But it's also a rich and versatile language, useful in a remarkable number of cases. We hope you'll find it as valuable as we do.

Acknowledgments

We are deeply indebted to friends who made comments and suggestions on drafts of this book. We are particularly grateful to Jon Bentley, whose enthusiasm has been an inspiration for years. Jon contributed many ideas and programs derived from his experience using and teaching awk; he also read several drafts with great care. Doug McIlroy also deserves special recognition; his peerless talent as a reader greatly improved the structure and content of the whole book. Others who made helpful comments on the manuscript include Susan Aho, Jaap Akkerhuis, Lorinda Cherry, Chris Fraser, Eric Grosse, Riccardo Gusella, Bob Herbst, Mark Kernighan, John Linderman, Bob Martin, Howard Moscovitz, Gerard Schmitt, Don Swartwout, Howard Trickey, Peter van Eijk, Chris Van Wyk, and Mihalis Yannakakis. We thank them all.

Alfred V. Aho
Brian W. Kernighan
Peter J. Weinberger

CONTENTS

1   AN AWK TUTORIAL

Awk is a convenient and expressive programming language that can be applied to a wide variety of computing and data-manipulation tasks. This chapter is a tutorial, designed to let you start writing your own programs as quickly as possible. Chapter 2 describes the whole language, and the remaining chapters show how awk can be used to solve problems from many different areas. Throughout the book, we have tried to pick examples that you should find useful, interesting, and instructive.

1.1   Getting Started

Useful awk programs are often short, just a line or two. Suppose you have a file called `emp.data` that contains the name, pay rate in dollars per hour, and number of hours worked for your employees, one employee record per line, like this:

```
Beth    4.00    0
Dan     3.75    0
Kathy   4.00    10
Mark    5.00    20
Mary    5.50    22
Susie   4.25    18
```

Now you want to print the name and pay (rate times hours) for everyone who worked more than zero hours. This is the kind of job that awk is meant for, so it's easy. Just type this command line:

```
awk '$3 > 0 { print $1, $2 * $3 }' emp.data
```

You should get this output:

```
Kathy 40
Mark 100
Mary 121
Susie 76.5
```

This command line tells the system to run awk, using the program inside the quote characters, taking its data from the input file `emp.data`. The part inside the quotes is the complete awk program. It consists of a single *pattern-action statement*. The pattern, `$3 > 0`, matches every input line in which the third column, or *field*, is greater than zero, and the action

```
{ print $1, $2 * $3 }
```

prints the first field and the product of the second and third fields of each matched line.

   If you want to print the names of those employees who did not work, type this command line:

```
awk '$3 == 0 { print $1 }' emp.data
```

Here the pattern, `$3 == 0`, matches each line in which the third field is equal to zero, and the action

```
{ print $1 }
```

prints its first field.

   As you read this book, try running and modifying the programs that are presented. Since most of the programs are short, you'll quickly get an under-standing of how awk works. On a Unix system, the two transactions above would look like this on the terminal:

```
$ awk '$3 > 0 { print $1, $2 * $3 }' emp.data
Kathy 40
Mark 100
Mary 121
Susie 76.5
$ awk '$3 == 0 { print $1 }' emp.data
Beth
Dan
$
```

The `$` at the beginning of a line is the prompt from the system; it may be different on your machine.

The Structure of an AWK Program

   Let's step back a moment and look at what is going on. In the command lines above, the parts between the quote characters are programs written in the awk programming language. Each awk program in this chapter is a sequence of one or more pattern-action statements:

```
pattern   { action }
pattern   { action }
. . .
```

The basic operation of awk is to scan a sequence of input lines one after another, searching for lines that are *matched* by any of the patterns in the program. The precise meaning of the word "match" depends on the pattern in question; for patterns like $3 > 0, it means "the condition is true."

Every input line is tested against each of the patterns in turn. For each pattern that matches, the corresponding action (which may involve multiple steps) is performed. Then the next line is read and the matching starts over. This continues until all the input has been read.

The programs above are typical examples of patterns and actions.

```
$3 == 0   { print $1 }
```

is a single pattern-action statement; for every line in which the third field is zero, the first field is printed.

Either the pattern or the action (but not both) in a pattern-action statement may be omitted. If a pattern has no action, for example,

```
$3 == 0
```

then each line that the pattern matches (that is, each line for which the condition is true) is printed. This program prints the two lines from the emp.data file where the third field is zero:

```
Beth    4.00    0
Dan     3.75    0
```

If there is an action with no pattern, for example,

```
{ print $1 }
```

then the action, in this case printing the first field, is performed for every input line.

Since patterns and actions are both optional, actions are enclosed in braces to distinguish them from patterns.

Running an AWK Program

There are several ways to run an awk program. You can type a command line of the form

```
awk 'program' input files
```

to run the *program* on each of the specified input files. For example, you could type

```
awk '$3 == 0 { print $1 }' file1 file2
```

to print the first field of every line of file1 and file2 in which the third field is zero.

You can omit the input files from the command line and just type

```
awk 'program'
```

In this case awk will apply the *program* to whatever you type next on your terminal until you type an end-of-file signal (control-d on Unix systems). Here is a sample of a session on Unix:

```
$ awk '$3 == 0 { print $1 }'
Beth     4.00     0
Beth
Dan      3.75     0
Dan
Kathy    3.75     10
Kathy    3.75     0
Kathy
...
```

The **heavy** characters are what the computer printed.

This behavior makes it easy to experiment with awk: type your program, then type data at it and see what happens. We again encourage you to try the examples and variations on them.

Notice that the program is enclosed in single quotes on the command line. This protects characters like $ in the program from being interpreted by the shell and also allows the program to be longer than one line.

This arrangement is convenient when the program is short (a few lines). If the program is long, however, it is more convenient to put it into a separate file, say `progfile`, and type the command line

```
awk -f progfile    optional list of input files
```

The `-f` option instructs awk to fetch the program from the named file. Any filename can be used in place of `progfile`.

Errors

If you make an error in an awk program, awk will give you a diagnostic message. For example, if you mistype a brace, like this:

```
awk '$3 == 0 [ print $1 }' emp.data
```

you will get a message like this:

```
awk: syntax error at source line 1
 context is
        $3 == 0 >>>  [ <<<
        extra }
        missing ]
awk: bailing out at source line 1
```

"Syntax error" means that you have made a grammatical error that was detected at the place marked by >>> <<<. "Bailing out" means that no recovery was attempted. Sometimes you get a little more help about what the error was, such as a report of mismatched braces or parentheses.

Because of the syntax error, awk did not try to execute this program. Some errors, however, may not be detected until your program is running. For example, if you attempt to divide a number by zero, awk will stop its processing and report the input line number and the line number in the program at which the division was attempted.

1.2 Simple Output

The rest of this chapter contains a collection of short, typical awk programs based on manipulation of the `emp.data` file above. We'll explain briefly what's going on, but these examples are meant mainly to suggest useful operations that are easy to do with awk — printing fields, selecting input, and transforming data. We are not showing everything that awk can do by any means, nor are we going into many details about the specific things presented here. But by the end of this chapter, you will be able to accomplish quite a bit, and you'll find it much easier to read the later chapters.

We will usually show just the program, not the whole command line. In every case, the program can be run either by enclosing it in quotes as the first argument of the `awk` command, as shown above, or by putting it in a file and invoking awk on that file with the `-f` option.

There are only two types of data in awk: numbers and strings of characters. The `emp.data` file is typical of this kind of information — a mixture of words and numbers separated by blanks and/or tabs.

Awk reads its input one line at a time and splits each line into fields, where, by default, a field is a sequence of characters that doesn't contain any blanks or tabs. The first field in the current input line is called `$1`, the second `$2`, and so forth. The entire line is called `$0`. The number of fields can vary from line to line.

Often, all we need to do is print some or all of the fields of each line, perhaps performing some calculations. The programs in this section are all of that form.

Printing Every Line

If an action has no pattern, the action is performed for all input lines. The statement `print` by itself prints the current input line, so the program

```
{ print }
```

prints all of its input on the standard output. Since `$0` is the whole line,

```
{ print $0 }
```

does the same thing.

Printing Certain Fields

More than one item can be printed on the same output line with a single `print` statement. The program to print the first and third fields of each input line is

```
{ print $1, $3 }
```

With `emp.data` as input, it produces

```
Beth 0
Dan 0
Kathy 10
Mark 20
Mary 22
Susie 18
```

Expressions separated by a comma in a `print` statement are, by default, separated by a single blank when they are printed. Each line produced by `print` ends with a newline character. Both of these defaults can be changed; we'll show how in Chapter 2.

NF, the Number of Fields

It might appear you must always refer to fields as $1, $2, and so on, but any expression can be used after $ to denote a field number; the expression is evaluated and its numeric value is used as the field number. Awk counts the number of fields in the current input line and stores the count in a built-in variable called NF. Thus, the program

```
{ print NF, $1, $NF }
```

prints the number of fields and the first and last fields of each input line.

Computing and Printing

You can also do computations on the field values and include the results in what is printed. The program

```
{ print $1, $2 * $3 }
```

is a typical example. It prints the name and total pay (rate times hours) for each employee:

```
Beth 0
Dan 0
Kathy 40
Mark 100
Mary 121
Susie 76.5
```

We'll show in a moment how to make this output look better.

Printing Line Numbers

Awk provides another built-variable, called NR, that counts the number of lines read so far. We can use NR and $0 to prefix each line of emp.data with its line number:

```
{ print NR, $0 }
```

The output looks like this:

```
1 Beth   4.00    0
2 Dan    3.75    0
3 Kathy  4.00    10
4 Mark   5.00    20
5 Mary   5.50    22
6 Susie  4.25    18
```

Putting Text in the Output

You can also print words in the midst of fields and computed values:

```
{ print "total pay for", $1, "is", $2 * $3 }
```

prints

```
total pay for Beth is 0
total pay for Dan is 0
total pay for Kathy is 40
total pay for Mark is 100
total pay for Mary is 121
total pay for Susie is 76.5
```

In the print statement, the text inside the double quotes is printed along with the fields and computed values.

1.3 Fancier Output

The print statement is meant for quick and easy output. To format the output exactly the way you want it, you may have to use the printf statement. As we shall see in Section 2.4, printf can produce almost any kind of output, but in this section we'll only show a few of its capabilities.

Lining Up Fields

The printf statement has the form

$$printf(format, value_1, value_2, ... , value_n)$$

where *format* is a string that contains text to be printed verbatim, interspersed with specifications of how each of the values is to be printed. A specification is a % followed by a few characters that control the format of a *value*. The first specification tells how $value_1$ is to be printed, the second how $value_2$ is to be printed, and so on. Thus, there must be as many % specifications in *format* as *value*s to be printed.

Here's a program that uses printf to print the total pay for every employee:

```
{ printf("total pay for %s is $%.2f\n", $1, $2 * $3) }
```

The specification string in the printf statement contains two % specifications.

The first, %s, says to print the first value, $1, as a string of characters; the second, %.2f, says to print the second value, $2*$3, as a number with 2 digits after the decimal point. Everything else in the specification string, including the dollar sign, is printed verbatim; the \n at the end of the string stands for a new-line, which causes subsequent output to begin on the next line. With emp.data as input, this program yields:

```
total pay for Beth is $0.00
total pay for Dan is $0.00
total pay for Kathy is $40.00
total pay for Mark is $100.00
total pay for Mary is $121.00
total pay for Susie is $76.50
```

With printf, no blanks or newlines are produced automatically; you must create them yourself. Don't forget the \n.

Here's another program that prints each employee's name and pay:

```
{ printf("%-8s $%6.2f\n", $1, $2 * $3) }
```

The first specification, %-8s, prints a name as a string of characters left-justified in a field 8 characters wide. The second specification, %6.2f, prints the pay as a number with two digits after the decimal point, in a field 6 characters wide:

```
Beth      $  0.00
Dan       $  0.00
Kathy     $ 40.00
Mark      $100.00
Mary      $121.00
Susie     $ 76.50
```

We'll show lots more examples of printf as we go along; the full story is in Section 2.4.

Sorting the Output

Suppose you want to print all the data for each employee, along with his or her pay, sorted in order of increasing pay. The easiest way is to use awk to pre-fix the total pay to each employee record, and run that output through a sorting program. On Unix, the command line

```
awk '{ printf("%6.2f  %s\n", $2 * $3, $0) }' emp.data | sort
```

pipes the output of awk into the sort command, and produces:

```
  0.00   Beth    4.00    0
  0.00   Dan     3.75    0
 40.00   Kathy   4.00    10
 76.50   Susie   4.25    18
100.00   Mark    5.00    20
121.00   Mary    5.50    22
```

1.4 Selection

Awk patterns are good for selecting interesting lines from the input for further processing. Since a pattern without an action prints all lines matching the pattern, many awk programs consist of nothing more than a single pattern. This section gives some examples of useful patterns.

Selection by Comparison

This program uses a comparison pattern to select the records of employees who earn $5.00 or more per hour, that is, lines in which the second field is greater than or equal to 5:

```
$2 >= 5
```

It selects these lines from emp.data:

```
Mark    5.00    20
Mary    5.50    22
```

Selection by Computation

The program

```
$2 * $3 > 50 { printf("$%.2f for %s\n", $2 * $3, $1) }
```

prints the pay of those employees whose total pay exceeds $50:

```
$100.00 for Mark
$121.00 for Mary
$76.50 for Susie
```

Selection by Text Content

Besides numeric tests, you can select input lines that contain specific words or phrases. This program prints all lines in which the first field is Susie:

```
$1 == "Susie"
```

The operator == tests for equality. You can also look for text containing any of a set of letters, words, and phrases by using patterns called *regular expressions*. This program prints all lines that contain Susie anywhere:

```
/Susie/
```

The output is this line:

```
Susie    4.25      18
```

Regular expressions can be used to specify much more elaborate patterns; Section 2.1 contains a full discussion.

Combinations of Patterns

Patterns can be combined with parentheses and the logical operators &&, ¦¦, and !, which stand for AND, OR, and NOT. The program

```
$2 >= 4 ¦¦ $3 >= 20
```

prints those lines where $2 is at least 4 *or* $3 is at least 20:

```
Beth     4.00      0
Kathy    4.00      10
Mark     5.00      20
Mary     5.50      22
Susie    4.25      18
```

Lines that satisfy both conditions are printed only once. Contrast this with the following program, which consists of two patterns:

```
$2 >= 4
$3 >= 20
```

This program prints an input line twice if it satisfies both conditions:

```
Beth     4.00      0
Kathy    4.00      10
Mark     5.00      20
Mark     5.00      20
Mary     5.50      22
Mary     5.50      22
Susie    4.25      18
```

Note that the program

```
!($2 < 4 && $3 < 20)
```

prints lines where it is *not* true that $2 is less than 4 *and* $3 is less than 20; this condition is equivalent to the first one above, though perhaps less readable.

Data Validation

There are always errors in real data. Awk is an excellent tool for checking that data has reasonable values and is in the right format, a task that is often called *data validation*.

Data validation is essentially negative: instead of printing lines with desirable properties, one prints lines that are suspicious. The following program uses comparison patterns to apply five plausibility tests to each line of `emp.data`:

```
NF != 3    { print $0, "number of fields is not equal to 3" }
$2 < 3.35 { print $0, "rate is below minimum wage" }
$2 > 10    { print $0, "rate exceeds $10 per hour" }
$3 < 0     { print $0, "negative hours worked" }
$3 > 60    { print $0, "too many hours worked" }
```

If there are no errors, there's no output.

BEGIN and END

The special pattern BEGIN matches before the first line of the first input file is read, and END matches after the last line of the last file has been processed. This program uses BEGIN to print a heading:

```
BEGIN { print "NAME    RATE    HOURS";  print "" }
      { print }
```

The output is:

```
NAME    RATE    HOURS

Beth    4.00    0
Dan     3.75    0
Kathy   4.00    10
Mark    5.00    20
Mary    5.50    22
Susie   4.25    18
```

You can put several statements on a single line if you separate them by semi-colons. Notice that `print ""` prints a blank line, quite different from just plain `print`, which prints the current input line.

1.5   Computing with AWK

An action is a sequence of statements separated by newlines or semicolons. You have already seen examples in which the action was a single `print` statement. This section provides examples of statements for performing simple numeric and string computations. In these statements you can use not only the built-in variables like NF, but you can create your own variables for performing calculations, storing data, and the like. In awk, user-created variables are not declared.

Counting

This program uses a variable `emp` to count employees who have worked more than 15 hours:

```
$3 > 15 { emp = emp + 1 }
END      { print emp, "employees worked more than 15 hours" }
```

For every line in which the third field exceeds 15, the previous value of emp is incremented by 1. With emp.data as input, this program yields:

```
3 employees worked more than 15 hours
```

Awk variables used as numbers begin life with the value 0, so we didn't need to initialize emp.

Computing Sums and Averages

To count the number of employees, we can use the built-in variable NR, which holds the number of lines read so far; its value at the end of all input is the total number of lines read.

```
END { print NR, "employees" }
```

The output is:

```
6 employees
```

Here is a program that uses NR to compute the average pay:

```
    { pay = pay + $2 * $3 }
END { print NR, "employees"
      print "total pay is", pay
      print "average pay is", pay/NR
    }
```

The first action accumulates the total pay for all employees. The END action prints

```
6 employees
total pay is 337.5
average pay is 56.25
```

Clearly, printf could be used to produce neater output. There's also a potential error: in the unlikely case that NR is zero, the program will attempt to divide by zero and thus will generate an error message.

Handling Text

One of the strengths of awk is its ability to handle strings of characters as conveniently as most languages handle numbers. Awk variables can hold strings of characters as well as numbers. This program finds the employee who is paid the most per hour:

```
$2 > maxrate { maxrate = $2; maxemp = $1 }
END { print "highest hourly rate:", maxrate, "for", maxemp }
```

It prints

```
highest hourly rate: 5.50 for Mary
```

In this program the variable `maxrate` holds a numeric value, while the variable `maxemp` holds a string. (If there are several employees who all make the same maximum pay, this program finds only the first.)

String Concatenation

New strings may be created by combining old ones; this operation is called *concatenation*. The program

```
    { names = names $1 " " }
END { print names }
```

collects all the employee names into a single string, by appending each name and a blank to the previous value in the variable `names`. The value of `names` is printed by the END action:

```
Beth Dan Kathy Mark Mary Susie
```

The concatenation operation is represented in an awk program by writing string values one after the other. At every input line, the first statement in the program concatenates three strings: the previous value of `names`, the first field, and a blank; it then assigns the resulting string to `names`. Thus, after all input lines have been read, `names` contains a single string consisting of the names of all the employees, each followed by a blank. Variables used to store strings begin life holding the null string (that is, the string containing no characters), so in this program `names` did not need to be explicitly initialized.

Printing the Last Input Line

Although NR retains its value in an END action, $0 does not. The program

```
    { last = $0 }
END { print last }
```

is one way to print the last input line:

```
Susie    4.25    18
```

Built-in Functions

We have already seen that awk provides built-in variables that maintain frequently used quantities like the number of fields and the input line number. Similarly, there are built-in functions for computing other useful values. Besides arithmetic functions for square roots, logarithms, random numbers, and the like, there are also functions that manipulate text. One of these is `length`, which counts the number of characters in a string. For example, this program computes the length of each person's name:

```
{ print $1, length($1) }
```

The result:

```
Beth  4
Dan   3
Kathy 5
Mark  4
Mary  4
Susie 5
```

Counting Lines, Words, and Characters

This program uses `length`, `NF`, and `NR` to count the number of lines, words, and characters in the input. For convenience, we'll treat each field as a word.

```
{ nc = nc + length($0) + 1
  nw = nw + NF
}
END { print NR, "lines,", nw, "words,", nc, "characters" }
```

The file `emp.data` has

```
6 lines, 18 words, 77 characters
```

We have added one for the newline character at the end of each input line, since `$0` doesn't include it.

1.6   Control-Flow Statements

Awk provides an `if-else` statement for making decisions and several statements for writing loops, all modeled on those found in the C programming language. They can only be used in actions.

If-Else Statement

The following program computes the total and average pay of employees making more than $6.00 an hour. It uses an `if` to defend against division by zero in computing the average pay.

```
$2 > 6 { n = n + 1; pay = pay + $2 * $3 }
END    { if (n > 0)
             print n, "employees, total pay is", pay,
                   "average pay is", pay/n
         else
             print "no employees are paid more than $6/hour"
       }
```

The output for `emp.data` is:

```
no employees are paid more than $6/hour
```

In the if-else statement, the condition following the if is evaluated. If it is true, the first print statement is performed. Otherwise, the second print statement is performed. Note that we can continue a long statement over several lines by breaking it after a comma.

While Statement

A while statement has a condition and a body. The statements in the body are performed repeatedly while the condition is true. This program shows how the value of an amount of money invested at a particular interest rate grows over a number of years, using the formula $value = amount\ (1+rate)^{years}$.

```
# interest1 - compute compound interest
#   input:  amount   rate   years
#   output: compounded value at the end of each year

{   i = 1
    while (i <= $3) {
        printf("\t%.2f\n", $1 * (1 + $2) ^ i)
        i = i + 1
    }
}
```

The condition is the parenthesized expression after the while; the loop body is the two statements enclosed in braces after the condition. The \t in the printf specification string stands for a tab character; the ^ is the exponentiation operator. Text from a # to the end of the line is a *comment*, which is ignored by awk but should be helpful to readers of the program who want to understand what is going on.

You can type triplets of numbers at this program to see what various amounts, rates, and years produce. For example, this transaction shows how $1000 grows at 6% and 12% compound interest for five years:

```
$ awk -f interest1
1000 .06 5
        1060.00
        1123.60
        1191.02
        1262.48
        1338.23
1000 .12 5
        1120.00
        1254.40
        1404.93
        1573.52
        1762.34
```

For Statement

Another statement, for, compresses into a single line the initialization, test, and increment that are part of most loops. Here is the previous interest computation with a for:

```
# interest2 - compute compound interest
#    input:  amount  rate  years
#    output: compounded value at the end of each year

{   for (i = 1; i <= $3; i = i + 1)
        printf("\t%.2f\n", $1 * (1 + $2) ^ i)
}
```

The initialization i = 1 is performed once. Next, the condition i <= $3 is tested; if it is true, the printf statement, which is the body of the loop, is performed. Then the increment i = i + 1 is performed after the body, and the next iteration of the loop begins with another test of the condition. The code is more compact, and since the body of the loop is only a single statement, no braces are needed to enclose it.

1.7 Arrays

Awk provides arrays for storing groups of related values. Although arrays give awk considerable power, we will show only a simple example here. The following program prints its input in reverse order by line. The first action puts the input lines into successive elements of the array line; that is, the first line goes into line[1], the second line into line[2], and so on. The END action uses a while statement to print the lines from the array from last to first:

```
# reverse - print input in reverse order by line

    { line[NR] = $0 }  # remember each input line

END { i = NR               # print lines in reverse order
      while (i > 0) {
          print line[i]
          i = i - 1
      }
    }
```

With emp.data, the output is

```
Susie   4.25    18
Mary    5.50    22
Mark    5.00    20
Kathy   4.00    10
Dan     3.75    0
Beth    4.00    0
```

Here is the same example with a `for` statement:

```
# reverse - print input in reverse order by line

    { line[NR] = $0 }  # remember each input line

END { for (i = NR; i > 0; i = i - 1)
        print line[i]
    }
```

1.8 A Handful of Useful "One-liners"

Although awk can be used to write programs of some complexity, many useful programs are not much more complicated than what we've seen so far. Here is a collection of short programs that you might find handy and/or instructive. Most are variations on material already covered.

1. Print the total number of input lines:

```
END { print NR }
```

2. Print the tenth input line:

```
NR == 10
```

3. Print the last field of every input line:

```
{ print $NF }
```

4. Print the last field of the last input line:

```
      { field = $NF}
END { print field }
```

5. Print every input line with more than four fields:

```
NF > 4
```

6. Print every input line in which the last field is more than 4:

```
$NF > 4
```

7. Print the total number of fields in all input lines:

```
      { nf = nf + NF }
END { print nf }
```

8. Print the total number of lines that contain Beth:

```
/Beth/ { nlines = nlines + 1 }
END      { print nlines }
```

9. Print the largest first field and the line that contains it (assumes some $1 is positive):

```
$1 > max { max = $1; maxline = $0 }
END      { print max, maxline }
```

10. Print every line that has at least one field:

```
NF > 0
```

11. Print every line longer than 80 characters:

```
length($0) > 80
```

12. Print the number of fields in every line followed by the line itself:

```
{ print NF, $0 }
```

13. Print the first two fields, in opposite order, of every line:

```
{ print $2, $1 }
```

14. Exchange the first two fields of every line and then print the line:

```
{ temp = $1; $1 = $2; $2 = temp; print }
```

15. Print every line with the first field replaced by the line number:

```
{ $1 = NR; print }
```

16. Print every line after erasing the second field:

```
{ $2 = ""; print }
```

17. Print in reverse order the fields of every line:

```
{ for (i = NF; i > 0; i = i - 1) printf("%s ", $i)
  printf("\n")
}
```

18. Print the sums of the fields of every line:

```
{ sum = 0
  for (i = 1; i <= NF; i = i + 1) sum = sum + $i
  print sum
}
```

19. Add up all fields in all lines and print the sum:

```
    { for (i = 1; i <= NF; i = i + 1) sum = sum + $i }
END { print sum }
```

20. Print every line after replacing each field by its absolute value:

```
{ for (i = 1; i <= NF; i = i + 1) if ($i < 0) $i = -$i
  print
}
```

1.9 What Next?

You have now seen the essentials of awk. Each program in this chapter has been a sequence of pattern-action statements. Awk tests every input line against the patterns, and when a pattern matches, performs the corresponding action. Patterns can involve numeric and string comparisons, and actions can include computation and formatted printing. Besides reading through your input files automatically, awk splits each input line into fields. It also provides a number of built-in variables and functions, and lets you define your own as well. With this combination of features, quite a few useful computations can be expressed by short programs — many of the details that would be needed in another language are handled implicitly in an awk program.

The rest of the book elaborates on these basic ideas. Since some of the examples are quite a bit bigger than anything in this chapter, we encourage you strongly to begin writing programs as soon as possible. This will give you familiarity with the language and make it easier to understand the larger programs. Furthermore, nothing answers questions so well as some simple experiments. You should also browse through the whole book; each example conveys something about the language, either about how to use a particular feature, or how to create an interesting program.

2   THE AWK LANGUAGE

This chapter explains, mostly with examples, the constructs that make up awk programs. Because it's a description of the complete language, the material is detailed, so we recommend that you skim it, then come back as necessary to check up on details.

The simplest awk program is a sequence of pattern-action statements:

```
pattern    { action }
pattern    { action }
. . .
```

In some statements, the pattern may be missing; in others, the action and its enclosing braces may be missing. After awk has checked your program to make sure there are no syntactic errors, it reads the input a line at a time, and for each line, evaluates the patterns in order. For each pattern that matches the current input line, it executes the associated action. A missing pattern matches every input line, so every action with no pattern is performed at each line. A pattern-action statement consisting only of a pattern prints each input line matched by the pattern. Throughout most of this chapter, the terms "input line" and "record" are used synonymously. In Section 2.5, we will discuss multiline records, where a record may contain several lines.

The first section of this chapter describes patterns in detail. The second section begins the description of actions by describing expressions, assignments, and control-flow statements. The remaining sections cover function definitions, output, input, and how awk programs can call other programs. Most sections contain summaries of major features.

The Input File countries

As input for many of the awk programs in this chapter, we will use a file called countries. Each line contains the name of a country, its area in thousands of square miles, its population in millions, and the continent it is in. The data is from 1984; the USSR has been arbitrarily placed in Asia. In the file, the four columns are separated by tabs; a single blank separates North and South from America.

The file countries contains the following lines:

```
USSR      8649    275     Asia
Canada    3852    25      North America
China     3705    1032    Asia
USA       3615    237     North America
Brazil    3286    134     South America
India     1267    746     Asia
Mexico    762     78      North America
France    211     55      Europe
Japan     144     120     Asia
Germany   96      61      Europe
England   94      56      Europe
```

For the rest of this chapter, the countries file is used when no input file is mentioned explicitly.

Program Format

Pattern-action statements and the statements within an action are usually separated by newlines, but several statements may appear on one line if they are separated by semicolons. A semicolon may be put at the end of any statement.

The opening brace of an action must be on the same line as the pattern it accompanies; the remainder of the action, including the closing brace, may appear on the following lines.

Blank lines are ignored; they may be inserted before or after any statement to improve the readability of a program. Blanks and tabs may be inserted around operators and operands, again to enhance readability.

Comments may be inserted at the end of any line. A comment starts with the character # and finishes at the end of the line, as in

```
{ print $1, $3 }    # print country name and population
```

A long statement may be spread over several lines by inserting a backslash and newline at each break:

```
{ print \
    $1,     # country name
    $2,     # area in thousands of square miles
    $3 }    # population in millions
```

As this example shows, statements may also be broken after commas, and a comment may be inserted at the end of each broken line.

In this book we have used several formatting styles, partly to illustrate different ones, and partly to keep programs from occupying too many lines. For short programs like those in this chapter, format doesn't much matter, but consistency and readability will help to keep longer programs manageable.

2.1 Patterns

Patterns control the execution of actions: when a pattern matches, its associated action is executed. This section describes the six types of patterns and the conditions under which they match.

Summary of Patterns

1. BEGIN { *statements* }
   The *statements* are executed once before any input has been read.

2. END { *statements* }
   The *statements* are executed once after all input has been read.

3. *expression* { *statements* }
   The *statements* are executed at each input line where the *expression* is true, that is, nonzero or nonnull.

4. */regular expression/* { *statements* }
   The *statements* are executed at each input line that contains a string matched by the *regular expression*.

5. *compound pattern* { *statements* }
   A compound pattern combines expressions with && (AND), ¦¦ (OR), ¦ (NOT), and parentheses; the *statements* are executed at each input line where the *compound pattern* is true.

6. *pattern*$_1$, *pattern*$_2$ { *statements* }
   A range pattern matches each input line from a line matched by *pattern*$_1$ to the next line matched by *pattern*$_2$, inclusive; the *statements* are executed at each matching line.

BEGIN and END do not combine with other patterns. A range pattern cannot be part of any other pattern. BEGIN and END are the only patterns that require an action.

BEGIN and END

The BEGIN and END patterns do not match any input lines. Rather, the statements in the BEGIN action are executed before awk reads any input; the statements in the END action are executed after all input has been read. BEGIN and END thus provide a way to gain control for initialization and wrapup. BEGIN and END do not combine with other patterns. If there is more than one BEGIN, the associated actions are executed in the order in which they appear in the program, and similarly for multiple END's. Although it's not mandatory, we put BEGIN first and END last.

One common use of a BEGIN action is to change the default way that input lines are split into fields. The field separator is controlled by a built-in variable

called FS. By default, fields are separated by blanks and/or tabs; this behavior
occurs when FS is set to a blank. Setting FS to any character other than a
blank makes that character the field separator.

The following program uses the BEGIN action to set the field separator to a
tab character (\t) and to put column headings on the output. The second
printf statement, which is executed at each input line, formats the output into
a table, neatly aligned under the column headings. The END action prints the
totals. (Variables and expressions are discussed in Section 2.2.)

```
# print countries with column headers and totals

BEGIN { FS = "\t"   # make tab the field separator
        printf("%10s %6s %5s    %s\n\n",
               "COUNTRY", "AREA", "POP", "CONTINENT")
      }
      { printf("%10s %6d %5d    %s\n", $1, $2, $3, $4)
        area = area + $2
        pop = pop + $3
      }
END   { printf("\n%10s %6d %5d\n", "TOTAL", area, pop) }
```

With the countries file as input, this program produces

```
COUNTRY    AREA   POP   CONTINENT

   USSR    8649   275   Asia
 Canada    3852    25   North America
  China    3705  1032   Asia
    USA    3615   237   North America
 Brazil    3286   134   South America
  India    1267   746   Asia
 Mexico     762    78   North America
 France     211    55   Europe
  Japan     144   120   Asia
Germany      96    61   Europe
England      94    56   Europe

  TOTAL   25681  2819
```

Expressions as Patterns

Like most programming languages, awk is rich in expressions for describing
numeric computations. Unlike many languages, awk also has expressions for
describing operations on strings. Throughout this book, the term *string* means a
sequence of zero or more characters. These may be stored in variables, or
appear literally as string constants like "" or "Asia". The string "", which
contains no characters, is called the *null string*. The term *substring* means a
contiguous sequence of zero or more characters within a string. In every string,
the null string appears as a substring of length zero before the first character,
between every pair of adjacent characters, and after the last character.

Any expression can be used as an operand of any operator. If an expression has a numeric value but an operator requires a string value, the numeric value is automatically transformed into a string; similarly, a string is converted into a number when an operator demands a numeric value.

Any expression can be used as a pattern. If an expression used as a pattern has a nonzero or nonnull value at the current input line, then the pattern matches that line. The typical expression patterns are those involving comparisons between numbers or strings. A comparison expression contains one of the six relational operators, or one of the two string-matching operators ~ (tilde) and !~ that will be discussed in the next section. These operators are listed in Table 2-1.

TABLE 2-1. COMPARISON OPERATORS

OPERATOR	MEANING
<	less than
<=	less than or equal to
==	equal to
!=	not equal to
>=	greater than or equal to
>	greater than
~	matched by
!~	not matched by

If the pattern is a comparison expression like NF>10, then it matches the current input line when the condition is satisfied, that is, when the number of fields in the line is greater than ten. If the pattern is an arithmetic expression like NF, it matches the current input line when its numeric value is nonzero. If the pattern is a string expression, it matches the current input line when the string value of the expression is nonnull.

In a relational comparison, if both operands are numeric, a numeric comparison is made; otherwise, any numeric operand is converted to a string, and then the operands are compared as strings. The strings are compared character by character using the ordering provided by the machine, most often the ASCII character set. One string is said to be "less than" another if it would appear before the other according to this ordering, e.g., "Canada" < "China" and "Asia" < "Asian".

The pattern

```
$3/$2 >= 0.5
```

selects lines where the value of the third field divided by the second is numerically greater than or equal to 0.5, while

```
$0 >= "M"
```

selects lines that begin with an M, N, O, etc.:

```
USSR     8649    275     Asia
USA      3615    237     North America
Mexico   762     78      North America
```

Sometimes the type of a comparison operator cannot be determined solely by the syntax of the expression in which it appears. The program

```
$1 < $4
```

could compare the first and fourth fields of each input line either as numbers or as strings. Here, the type of the comparison depends on the values of the fields, and it may vary from line to line. In the countries file, the first and fourth fields are always strings, so string comparisons are always made; the output is

```
Canada  3852    25      North America
Brazil  3286    134     South America
Mexico  762     78      North America
England 94      56      Europe
```

Only if both fields are numbers is the comparison done numerically; this would be the case with

```
$2 < $3
```

on the same data.

Section 2.2 contains a more complete discussion of strings, numbers, and expressions.

String-Matching Patterns

Awk provides a notation called *regular expressions* for specifying and matching strings of characters. Regular expressions are widely used in Unix programs, including its text editors and shell. Restricted forms of regular expressions also occur in systems like MS-DOS as "wild-card characters" for specifying sets of filenames.

A *string-matching pattern* tests whether a string contains a substring matched by a regular expression.

The simplest regular expression is a string of letters and numbers, like Asia, that matches itself. To turn a regular expression into a string-matching pattern, just enclose it in slashes:

```
/Asia/
```

This pattern matches when the current input line contains the substring Asia, either as Asia by itself or as some part of a larger word like Asian or Pan-Asiatic. Note that blanks are significant within regular expressions: the string-matching pattern

String-Matching Patterns

1. */regexpr/*
   Matches when the current input line contains a substring matched by *regexpr*.

2. *expression ~ /regexpr/*
   Matches if the string value of *expression* contains a substring matched by *regexpr*.

3. *expression !~ /regexpr/*
   Matches if the string value of *expression* does not contain a substring matched by *regexpr*.

Any expression may be used in place of */regexpr/* in the context of ~ and !~.

```
/ Asia /
```

matches only when `Asia` is surrounded by blanks.

The pattern above is one of three types of string-matching patterns. Its form is a regular expression *r* enclosed in slashes:

```
/r/
```

This pattern matches an input line if the line contains a substring matched by *r*.

The other two types of string-matching patterns use an explicit matching operator:

expression ~ /r/
expression !~ /r/

The matching operator ~ means "is matched by" and !~ means "is not matched by." The first pattern matches when the string value of *expression* contains a substring matched by the regular expression *r*; the second pattern matches if there is no such substring.

The left operand of a matching operator is often a field: the pattern

```
$4 ~ /Asia/
```

matches all input lines in which the fourth field contains `Asia` as a substring, while

```
$4 !~ /Asia/
```

matches if the fourth field does *not* contain `Asia` anywhere.

Note that the string-matching pattern

```
/Asia/
```

is a shorthand for

```
$0 ~ /Asia/
```

Regular Expressions

A regular expression is a notation for specifying and matching strings. Like an arithmetic expression, a regular expression is a basic expression or one created by applying operators to component expressions. To understand the strings matched by a regular expression, we need to understand the strings matched by its components.

Regular Expressions

1. The regular expression metacharacters are:

   \ ^ $. [ ] ¦ ( ) * + ?

2. A basic regular expression is one of the following:
   a nonmetacharacter, such as A, that matches itself.
   an escape sequence that matches a special symbol: \t matches a tab (see Table 2-2).
   a quoted metacharacter, such as *, that matches the metacharacter literally.
   ^, which matches the beginning of a string.
   $, which matches the end of a string.
   ., which matches any single character.
   a character class: [ABC] matches any of the characters A, B, or C.
   character classes may include abbreviations: [A-Za-z] matches any single letter.
   a complemented character class: [^0-9] matches any character except a digit.

3. These operators combine regular expressions into larger ones:
   alternation: A¦B matches A or B.
   concatenation: AB matches A immediately followed by B.
   closure: A* matches zero or more A's.
   positive closure: A+ matches one or more A's.
   zero or one: A? matches the null string or A.
   parentheses: (r) matches the same strings as r does.

The basic regular expressions are summarized in the table above. The characters

   \ ^ $. [ ] ¦ ( ) * + ?

are called *metacharacters* because they have special meanings. A regular expression consisting of a single nonmetacharacter matches itself. Thus, a single letter or digit is a basic regular expression that matches itself. To preserve the literal meaning of a metacharacter in a regular expression, precede it by a backslash. Thus, the regular expression \$ matches the character $. If a character is preceded by a single \, we'll say that character is *quoted*.

In a regular expression, an unquoted caret ^ matches the beginning of a string, an unquoted dollar-sign $ matches the end of a string, and an unquoted period . matches any single character. Thus,

`^C`	matches a C at the beginning of a string
`C$`	matches a C at the end of a string
`^C$`	matches the string consisting of the single character C
`^.$`	matches any string containing exactly one character
`^...$`	matches any string containing exactly three characters
`...`	matches any three consecutive characters
`\.$`	matches a period at the end of a string

A regular expression consisting of a group of characters enclosed in brackets is called a *character class*; it matches any one of the enclosed characters. For example, `[AEIOU]` matches any of the characters A, E, I, O, or U.

Ranges of characters can be abbreviated in a character class by using a hyphen. The character immediately to the left of the hyphen defines the beginning of the range; the character immediately to the right defines the end. Thus, `[0-9]` matches any digit, and `[a-zA-Z][0-9]` matches a letter followed by a digit. Without both a left and right operand, a hyphen in a character class denotes itself, so the character classes `[+-]` and `[-+]` match either a + or a -. The character class `[A-Za-z-]+` matches words that include hyphens.

A *complemented* character class is one in which the first character after the `[` is a `^`. Such a class matches any character *not* in the group following the caret. Thus, `[^0-9]` matches any character except a digit; `[^a-zA-Z]` matches any character except an upper or lower-case letter.

`^[ABC]`	matches an A, B or C at the beginning of a string
`^[^ABC]`	matches any character at the beginning of a string, except A, B or C
`[^ABC]`	matches any character other than an A, B or C
`^[^a-z]$`	matches any single-character string, except a lower-case letter

Inside a character class, all characters have their literal meaning, except for the quoting character `\`, `^` at the beginning, and `-` between two characters. Thus, `[.]` matches a period and `^[^^]` matches any character except a caret at the beginning of a string.

Parentheses are used in regular expressions to specify how components are grouped. There are two binary regular expression operators: alternation and concatenation. The alternation operator `|` is used to specify alternatives: if r_1 and r_2 are regular expressions, then $r_1 | r_2$ matches any string matched by r_1 or by r_2.

There is no explicit concatenation operator. If r_1 and r_2 are regular expressions, then $(r_1)(r_2)$ (with no blank between (r_1) and (r_2)) matches any string of the form xy where r_1 matches x and r_2 matches y. The parentheses around r_1 or r_2 can be omitted, if the contained regular expression does not contain the alternation operator. The regular expression

`(Asian|European|North American) (male|female) (black|blue)bird`

matches twelve strings ranging from

```
Asian male blackbird
```

to

```
North American female bluebird
```

The symbols *, +, and ? are unary operators used to specify repetitions in regular expressions. If *r* is a regular expression, then (*r*)* matches any string consisting of zero or more consecutive substrings matched by *r*, (*r*)+ matches any string consisting of one or more consecutive substrings matched by *r*, and (*r*)? matches the null string or any string matched by *r*. If *r* is a basic regular expression, then the parentheses can be omitted.

B*	matches the null string or B or BB, and so on
AB*C	matches AC or ABC or ABBC, and so on
AB+C	matches ABC or ABBC or ABBBC, and so on
ABB*C	also matches ABC or ABBC or ABBBC, and so on
AB?C	matches AC or ABC
[A-Z]+	matches any string of one or more upper-case letters
(AB)+C	matches ABC, ABABC, ABABABC, and so on

In regular expressions, the alternation operator ¦ has the lowest precedence, then concatenation, and finally the repetition operators *, +, and ?. As in arithmetic expressions, operators of higher precedence are done before lower ones. These conventions often allow parentheses to be omitted: ab¦cd is the same as (ab)¦(cd), and ^ab¦cd*e$ is the same as (^ab)¦(c(d*)e$).

To finish our discussion of regular expressions, here are some examples of useful string-matching patterns containing regular expressions with unary and binary operators, along with a description of the kinds of input lines they match. Recall that a string-matching pattern /*r*/ matches the current input line if the line contains at least one substring matched by *r*.

```
/^[0-9]+$/
        matches any input line that consists of only digits
/^[0-9][0-9][0-9]$/
        exactly three digits
/^(\+¦-)?[0-9]+\.?[0-9]*$/
        a decimal number with an optional sign and optional fraction
/^[+-]?[0-9]+[.]?[0-9]*$/
        also a decimal number with an optional sign and optional fraction
/^[+-]?([0-9]+[.]?[0-9]*¦[.][0-9]+)([eE][+-]?[0-9]+)?$/
        a floating point number with optional sign and optional exponent
/^[A-Za-z][A-Za-z0-9]*$/
        a letter followed by any letters or digits (e.g., awk variable name)
/^[A-Za-z]$¦^[A-Za-z][0-9]$/
        a letter or a letter followed by a digit (e.g., variable name in Basic)
/^[A-Za-z][0-9]?$/
        also a letter or a letter followed by a digit
```

Since + and . are metacharacters, they have to be preceded by backslashes in the third example to match literal occurrences. These backslashes are not

needed within character classes, so the fourth example shows an alternate way
to describe the same numbers.

Any regular expression enclosed in slashes can be used as the right-hand
operand of a matching operator: the program

```
$2 !~ /^[0-9]+$/
```

prints all lines in which the second field is not a string of digits.

Within regular expressions and strings, awk uses certain character sequences,
called *escape sequences*, to specify characters for which there may be no other
notation. For example, \n stands for a newline character, which cannot otherwise appear in a string or regular expression; \b stands for backspace; \t
stands for tab; \007 represents the ASCII bell character; and \/ represents a
slash. Escape sequences have special meaning only within an awk program;
they are just characters in data. The complete list of escape sequences is shown
in Table 2-2.

TABLE 2-2. ESCAPE SEQUENCES

SEQUENCE	MEANING
\b	backspace
\f	formfeed
\n	newline (line feed)
\r	carriage return
\t	tab
\ddd	octal value ddd, where ddd is 1 to 3 digits between 0 and 7
\c	any other character c literally (e.g., \\ for backslash, \" for ")

Table 2-3 summarizes regular expressions and the strings they match. The
operators are listed in order of increasing precedence.

Compound Patterns

A compound pattern is an expression that combines other patterns, using
parentheses and the logical operators ¦¦ (OR), && (AND), and ! (NOT). A
compound pattern matches the current input line if the expression evaluates to
true. The following program uses the AND operator to select all lines in which
the fourth field is Asia and the third field exceeds 500:

```
$4 == "Asia" && $3 > 500
```

The program

```
$4 == "Asia" ¦¦ $4 == "Europe"
```

uses the OR operator to select lines with either Asia or Europe as the fourth
field. Because the latter query is a test on string values, another way to write it

TABLE 2-3. REGULAR EXPRESSIONS

EXPRESSION	MATCHES
c	the nonmetacharacter c
\c	escape sequence or literal character c
^	beginning of string
$	end of string
.	any character
$[c_1c_2...]$	any character in $c_1c_2...$
$[\hat{\ }c_1c_2...]$	any character not in $c_1c_2...$
$[c_1-c_2]$	any character in the range beginning with c_1 and ending with c_2
$[\hat{\ }c_1-c_2]$	any character not in the range c_1 to c_2
$r_1 \mid r_2$	any string matched by r_1 or r_2
$(r_1)(r_2)$	any string xy where r_1 matches x and r_2 matches y; parentheses not needed around arguments with no alternations
$(r)*$	zero or more consecutive strings matched by r
$(r)+$	one or more consecutive strings matched by r
$(r)?$	zero or one string matched by r parentheses not needed around basic regular expressions
(r)	any string matched by r

is to use a regular expression with the alternation operator ¦:

```
$4 ~ /^(Asia¦Europe)$/
```

(Two regular expressions are *equivalent* if they match the same strings. Test your understanding of the precedence rules for regular expressions: Are the two regular expressions ^Asia¦Europe$ and ^(Asia¦Europe)$ equivalent?)

If there are no occurrences of Asia or Europe in other fields, this pattern could also be written as

```
/Asia/ ¦¦ /Europe/
```

or even

```
/Asia¦Europe/
```

The ¦¦ operator has the lowest precedence, then &&, and finally !. The && and ¦¦ operators evaluate their operands from left to right; evaluation stops as soon as truth or falsehood is determined.

Range Patterns

A range pattern consists of two patterns separated by a comma, as in

pat_1, pat_2

A range pattern matches each line between an occurrence of pat_1 and the next occurrence of pat_2 inclusive; pat_2 may match the same line as pat_1, making the range a single line. As an example, the pattern

```
/Canada/, /USA/
```

matches lines starting with the first line that contains Canada up through the next line that contains USA.

Matching begins whenever the first pattern of a range matches; if no instance of the second pattern is subsequently found, then all lines to the end of the input are matched:

```
/Europe/, /Africa/
```

prints

```
France   211      55       Europe
Japan    144      120      Asia
Germany  96       61       Europe
England  94       56       Europe
```

In the next example, FNR is the number of the line just read from the current input file and FILENAME is the filename itself; both are built-in variables. Thus, the program

```
FNR == 1, FNR == 5 { print FILENAME ": " $0 }
```

prints the first five lines of each input file with the filename prefixed. Alternately, this program could be written as

```
FNR <= 5 { print FILENAME ": " $0 }
```

A range pattern cannot be part of any other pattern.

Summary of Patterns

Table 2-4 summarizes the kinds of patterns that can appear in pattern-action statements.

TABLE 2-4. PATTERNS

PATTERN	EXAMPLE	MATCHES
BEGIN	BEGIN	before any input has been read
END	END	after all input has been read
expression	$3 < 100	lines in which third field is less than 100
string-matching	/Asia/	lines that contain Asia
compound	$3 < 100 &&	lines in which third field is less than 100 and
	$4 == "Asia"	fourth field is Asia
range	NR==10, NR==20	tenth to twentieth lines of input inclusive

2.2   Actions

In a pattern-action statement, the pattern determines when the action is to be executed. Sometimes an action is very simple: a single print or assignment. Other times, it may be a sequence of several statements separated by newlines or semicolons. This section begins the description of actions by discussing expressions and control-flow statements. The following sections present user-defined functions, and statements for input and output.

Actions

The statements in actions can include:

    expressions, with constants, variables, assignments, function calls, etc.
    print *expression-list*
    printf(*format*, *expression-list*)
    if (*expression*) *statement*
    if (*expression*) *statement* else *statement*
    while (*expression*) *statement*
    for (*expression*; *expression*; *expression*) *statement*
    for (*variable* in *array*) *statement*
    do *statement* while (*expression*)
    break
    continue
    next
    exit
    exit *expression*
    { *statements* }

Expressions

We begin with expressions, since expressions are the simplest statements, and most other statements are made up of expressions of various kinds. An expression is formed by combining primary expressions and other expressions with operators. The primary expressions are the primitive building blocks: they include constants, variables, array references, function invocations, and various built-ins, like field names.

Our discussion of expressions starts with constants and variables. Then come the operators that can be used to combine expressions. These operators fall into five categories: arithmetic, comparison, logical, conditional, and assignment. The built-in arithmetic and string functions come next, followed at the end of the section by the description of arrays.

Constants. There are two types of constants, string and numeric. A string constant is created by enclosing a sequence of characters in quotation marks, as in "Asia" or "hello, world" or "". String constants may contain the escape sequences listed in Table 2-2.

A numeric constant can be an integer like 1127, a decimal number like 3.14, or a number in scientific (exponential) notation like 0.707E-1. Different representations of the same number have the same numeric value: the numbers 1e6, 1.00E6, 10e5, 0.1e7, and 1000000 are numerically equal. All numbers are stored in floating point, the precision of which is machine dependent.

Variables. Expressions can contain several kinds of variables: user-defined, built-in, and fields. The names of user-defined variables are sequences of letters, digits, and underscores that do not begin with a digit; all built-in variables have upper-case names.

A variable has a value that is a string or a number or both. Since the type of a variable is not declared, awk infers the type from context. When necessary, awk will convert a string value into a numeric one, or vice versa. For example, in

```
$4 == "Asia" { print $1, 1000 * $2 }
```

$2 is converted into a number if it is not one already, and $1 and $4 are converted into strings if they are not already.

An uninitialized variable has the string value "" (the null string) and the numeric value 0.

Built-In Variables. Table 2-5 lists the built-in variables. Some of these we have already met; others will be used in this and later sections. These variables can be used in all expressions, and may be reset by the user. FILENAME is set each time a new file is read. FNR, NF, and NR are set each time a new record is read; additionally, NF is reset when $0 changes or when a new field is created. RLENGTH and RSTART change as a result of invoking the match function.

Field Variables. The fields of the current input line are called $1, $2, through $NF; $0 refers to the whole line. Fields share the properties of other variables — they may be used in arithmetic or string operations, and may be assigned to. Thus one can divide the second field in each line of countries by 1000 to express areas in millions of square miles instead of thousands:

```
{ $2 = $2 / 1000; print }
```

One can assign a new string to a field:

```
BEGIN                      { FS = OFS = "\t" }
$4 == "North America"      { $4 = "NA" }
$4 == "South America"      { $4 = "SA" }
                           { print }
```

In this program, the BEGIN action sets FS, the variable that controls the input field separator, and OFS, the output field separator, both to a tab. The print

TABLE 2-5. BUILT-IN VARIABLES

VARIABLE	MEANING	DEFAULT
ARGC	number of command-line arguments	-
ARGV	array of command-line arguments	-
FILENAME	name of current input file	-
FNR	record number in current file	-
FS	controls the input field separator	" "
NF	number of fields in current record	-
NR	number of records read so far	-
OFMT	output format for numbers	"%.6g"
OFS	output field separator	" "
ORS	output record separator	"\n"
RLENGTH	length of string matched by match function	-
RS	controls the input record separator	"\n"
RSTART	start of string matched by match function	-
SUBSEP	subscript separator	"\034"

statement in the fourth line prints the value of $0 after it has been modified by previous assignments. This is important: when $0 is changed by assignment or substitution, $1, $2, etc., and NF will be recomputed; likewise, when one of $1, $2, etc., is changed, $0 is reconstructed using OFS to separate fields.

Fields can also be specified by expressions. For example, $(NF-1) is the next-to-last field of the current line. The parentheses are needed: $NF-1 is one less than the numeric value of the last field.

A field variable referring to a nonexistent field, e.g., $(NF+1), has as its initial value the null string. A new field can be created by assigning a value to it. For example, the following program creates a fifth field containing the population density:

```
BEGIN    { FS = OFS = "\t" }
         { $5 = 1000 * $3 / $2; print }
```

Any intervening fields are created when necessary and given null values.

The number of fields can vary from line to line, but there is usually an implementation limit of 100 fields per line.

Arithmetic Operators. Awk provides the usual +, -, *, /, %, and ^ arithmetic operators. The % operator computes remainders: x%y is the remainder when x is divided by y; its behavior depends on the machine if x or y is negative. The ^ operator is exponentiation: x^y is x^y. All arithmetic is done in floating point.

Comparison Operators. Comparison expressions are those containing either a relational operator or a regular expression matching operator. The relational

Expressions

1. The primary expressions are:
   numeric and string constants, variables, fields, function calls, array elements.

2. These operators combine expressions:
   assignment operators = += -= *= /= %= ^=
   conditional expression operator ? :
   logical operators ¦¦ (OR), && (AND), ! (NOT)
   matching operators ~ and !~
   relational operators < <= == != > >=
   concatenation (no explicit operator)
   arithmetic operators + - * / % ^
   unary + and -
   increment and decrement operators ++ and -- (prefix and postfix)
   parentheses for grouping

operators are <, <=, == (equals), != (not equals), >=, and >. The regular expression matching operators are ~ (is matched by) and !~ (is not matched by). The value of a comparison expression is 1 if it is true and 0 otherwise.

Similarly, the value of a matching expression is 1 if true, 0 if false, so

> $4 ~ /Asia/

is 1 if the fourth field of the current line contains Asia as a substring, or 0 if it does not.

Logical Operators. The logical operators && (AND), ¦¦ (OR), and ! (NOT) are used to create logical expressions by combining other expressions. A logical expression has the value 1 if it is true and 0 if it is false. In the evaluation of a logical operator, an operand with a nonzero or nonnull value is treated as true; other values are treated as false. The operands of expressions separated by && or ¦¦ are evaluated from left to right, and evaluation ceases as soon as the value of the complete expression can be determined. This means that in

> $expr_1$ && $expr_2$

$expr_2$ is not evaluated if $expr_1$ is false, while in

> $expr_3$ ¦¦ $expr_4$

$expr_4$ is not evaluated if $expr_3$ is true.

Newlines may be inserted after the && and ¦¦ operators.

Conditional Expressions. A conditional expression has the form

> $expr_1$? $expr_2$: $expr_3$

First, $expr_1$ is evaluated. If it is true, that is, nonzero or nonnull, the value of the conditional expression is the value of $expr_2$; otherwise, it is the value of $expr_3$. Only one of $expr_2$ and $expr_3$ is evaluated.

The following program uses a conditional expression to print the reciprocal of $ 1, or a warning if $ 1 is zero:

```
{ print ($1 != 0 ? 1/$1 : "$1 is zero, line " NR) }
```

Assignment Operators. There are seven assignment operators that can be used in expressions called *assignments*. The simplest assignment is an expression of the form

>   *var* = *expr*

where *var* is a variable or field name, and *expr* is any expression. For example, to compute the total population and number of Asian countries, we could write

```
$4 == "Asia" { pop = pop + $3; n = n + 1 }
END          { print "Total population of the", n,
                     "Asian countries is", pop, "million."
             }
```

Applied to countries, the program produces

```
Total population of the 4 Asian countries is 2173 million.
```

The first action contains two assignments, one to accumulate population, and the other to count countries. The variables are not explicitly initialized, yet everything works properly because each variable is initialized by default to the string value " " and the numeric value 0.

We also use default initialization to advantage in the following program, which finds the country with the largest population:

```
$3 > maxpop  { maxpop = $3; country = $1 }
END          { print "country with largest population:",
                     country, maxpop
             }
```

Note, however, that this program is correct only when at least one value of $ 3 is positive.

The other six assignment operators are +=, -=, *=, /=, %=, and ^=. Their meanings are similar: *v op= e* has the same effect as *v = v op e*, except that *v* is evaluated only once. The assignment

```
pop = pop + $3
```

can be written more concisely using the assignment operator +=:

```
pop += $3
```

This statement has the same effect as the longer version — the variable on the left is incremented by the value of the expression on the right — but += is shorter and runs faster. As another example,

```
{ $2 /= 1000; print }
```

divides the second field by 1000, then prints the line.

An assignment is an expression; its value is the new value of the left side. Thus assignments can be used inside any expression. In the multiple assignment

```
FS = OFS = "\t"
```

both the field separator and the output field separator are set to tab. Assignment expressions are also common within tests, such as:

```
if ((n = length($0)) > 0) ...
```

Increment and Decrement Operators. The assignment

```
n = n + 1
```

is usually written ++n or n++ using the unary increment operator ++, which adds 1 to a variable. The prefix form ++n increments n before delivering its value; the postfix form n++ increments n after delivering its value. This makes a difference when ++ is used in an assignment. If n is initially 1, then the assignment i = ++n increments n and assigns the new value 2 to i, while the assignment i = n++ increments n but assigns the old value 1 to i. To just increment n, however, there's no difference between n++ and ++n. The prefix and postfix decrement operator --, which subtracts 1 from a variable, works the same way.

Built-In Arithmetic Functions. The built-in arithmetic functions are shown in Table 2-6. These functions can be used as primary expressions in all expressions. In the table, x and y are arbitrary expressions.

TABLE 2-6. BUILT-IN ARITHMETIC FUNCTIONS

FUNCTION	VALUE RETURNED
atan2(y,x)	arctangent of y/x in the range $-\pi$ to π
cos(x)	cosine of x, with x in radians
exp(x)	exponential function of x, e^x
int(x)	integer part of x; truncated towards 0 when $x > 0$
log(x)	natural (base e) logarithm of x
rand()	random number r, where $0 \leqslant r < 1$
sin(x)	sine of x, with x in radians
sqrt(x)	square root of x
srand(x)	x is new seed for rand()

Useful constants can be computed with these functions: atan2(0,-1) gives π and exp(1) gives e, the base of the natural logarithms. To compute the base-10 logarithm of x, use log(x)/log(10).

The function `rand()` returns a pseudo-random floating point number greater than or equal to 0 and less than 1. Calling `srand(x)` sets the starting point of the generator from x. Calling `srand()` sets the starting point from the time of day. If `srand` is not called, `rand` starts with the same value each time the program is run.

The assignment

```
randint = int(n * rand()) + 1
```

sets `randint` to a random integer between 1 and n inclusive. Here we are using the `int` function to discard the fractional part. The assignment

```
x = int(x + 0.5)
```

rounds the value of x to the nearest integer when x is positive.

String Operators. There is only one string operation, concatenation. It has no explicit operator: string expressions are created by writing constants, variables, fields, array elements, function values, and other expressions next to one another. The program

```
{ print NR ":" $0 }
```

prints each line preceded by its line number and a colon, with no blanks. The number NR is converted to its string value (and so is $0 if necessary); then the three strings are concatenated and the result is printed.

Strings as Regular Expressions. So far, in all of our examples of matching expressions, the right-hand operand of ~ and ! ~ has been a regular expression enclosed in slashes. But, in fact, any expression can be used as the right operand of these operators. Awk evaluates the expression, converts the value to a string if necessary, and interprets the string as a regular expression. For example, the program

```
BEGIN    { digits = "^[0-9]+$" }
$2 ~ digits
```

will print all lines in which the second field is a string of digits.

Since expressions can be concatenated, a regular expression can be built up from components. The following program echoes input lines that are valid floating point numbers:

```
BEGIN {
    sign = "[+-]?"
    decimal = "[0-9]+[.]?[0-9]*"
    fraction = "[.][0-9]+"
    exponent = "([eE]" sign "[0-9]+)?"
    number = "^" sign "(" decimal "|" fraction ")" exponent "$"
}
$0 ~ number
```

In a matching expression, a quoted string like `"^[0-9]+$"` can normally be

used interchangeably with a regular expression enclosed in slashes, such as
/^[0-9]+$/. There is one exception, however. If the string in quotes is to
match a literal occurrence of a regular expression metacharacter, one extra
backslash is needed to protect the protecting backslash itself. That is,

```
$0 ~ /(\+|-)[0-9]+/
```

and

```
$0 ~ "(\\+|-)[0-9]+"
```

are equivalent.

This behavior may seem arcane, but it arises because one level of protecting
backslashes is removed when a quoted string is parsed by awk. If a backslash is
needed in front of a metacharacter to turn off its special meaning in a regular
expression, then that backslash needs a preceding backslash to protect it in a
string. If the right operand of a matching operator is a variable or field variable, as in

```
x ~ $1
```

then the additional level of backslashes is not needed in the first field because
backslashes have no special meaning in data.

As an aside, it's easy to test your understanding of regular expressions
interactively: the program

```
$1 ~ $2
```

lets you type in a string and a regular expression; it echoes the line back if the
string matches the regular expression.

Built-In String Functions. Awk provides the built-in string functions shown
in Table 2-7. In this table, *r* represents a regular expression (either as a string
or enclosed in slashes), *s* and *t* are string expressions, and *n* and *p* are integers.

The function index(s,t) returns the leftmost position where the string *t*
begins in *s*, or zero if *t* does not occur in *s*. The first character in a string is at
position 1:

```
index("banana", "an")
```

returns 2.

The function match(s,r) finds the leftmost longest substring in the string *s*
that is matched by the regular expression *r*. It returns the index where the substring begins or 0 if there is no matching substring. It also sets the built-in
variables RSTART to this index and RLENGTH to the length of the matched substring.

The function split(s,a,fs) splits the string *s* into the array *a* according
to the separator *fs* and returns the number of elements. It is described after
arrays, at the end of this section.

TABLE 2-7. BUILT-IN STRING FUNCTIONS

FUNCTION	DESCRIPTION
gsub(r,s)	substitute s for r globally in $0, return number of substitutions made
gsub(r,s,t)	substitute s for r globally in string t, return number of substitutions made
index(s,t)	return first position of string t in s, or 0 if t is not present
length(s)	return number of characters in s
match(s,r)	test whether s contains a substring matched by r; return index or 0; sets RSTART and RLENGTH
split(s,a)	split s into array a on FS, return number of fields
split(s,a,fs)	split s into array a on field separator fs, return number of fields
sprintf(fmt,expr-list)	return expr-list formatted according to format string fmt
sub(r,s)	substitute s for the leftmost longest substring of $0 matched by r; return number of substitutions made
sub(r,s,t)	substitute s for the leftmost longest substring of t matched by r; return number of substitutions made
substr(s,p)	return suffix of s starting at position p
substr(s,p,n)	return substring of s of length n starting at position p

The string function $\texttt{sprintf}(format, expr_1, expr_2, \ldots, expr_n)$ returns (without printing) a string containing $expr_1, expr_2, \ldots, expr_n$ formatted according to the printf specifications in the string value of the expression *format*. Thus, the statement

```
x = sprintf("%10s %6d", $1, $2)
```

assigns to x the string produced by formatting the values of $1 and $2 as a ten-character string and a decimal number in a field of width at least six. Section 2.4 contains a complete description of the format-conversion characters.

The functions sub and gsub are patterned after the substitute command in the Unix text editor ed. The function sub(r,s,t) first finds the leftmost longest substring matched by the regular expression r in the target string t; it then replaces the substring by the substitution string s. As in ed, "leftmost longest" means that the leftmost match is found first, then extended as far as possible.

In the target string banana, for example, anan is the leftmost longest substring matched by the regular expression (an)+. By contrast, the leftmost longest match of (an)* is the null string before b.

The sub function returns the number of substitutions made. The function sub(r,s) is a synonym for sub(r,s,$0).

The function gsub(r,s,t) is similar, except that it successively replaces the leftmost longest nonoverlapping substrings matched by *r* with *s* in *t*; it returns the number of substitutions made. (The "g" is for "global," meaning everywhere.) For example, the program

```
{ gsub(/USA/, "United States"); print }
```

will transcribe its input, replacing all occurrences of "USA" by "United States". (In such examples, when $0 changes, the fields and NF change too.) And

```
gsub(/ana/, "anda", "banana")
```

will replace banana by bandana; matches are nonoverlapping.

In a substitution performed by either sub(*r*,*s*,*t*) or gsub(*r*,*s*,*t*), any occurrence of the character & in *s* will be replaced by the substring matched by *r*. Thus

```
gsub(/a/, "aba", "banana")
```

replaces banana by babanabanaba; so does

```
gsub(/a/, "&b&", "banana")
```

The special meaning of & in the substitution string can be turned off by preceding it with a backslash, as in \&.

The function substr(*s*,*p*) returns the suffix of *s* that begins at position *p*. If substr(*s*,*p*,*n*) is used, only the first *n* characters of the suffix are returned; if the suffix is shorter than *n*, then the entire suffix is returned. For example, we could abbreviate the country names in countries to their first three characters by the program

```
{ $1 = substr($1, 1, 3); print $0 }
```

to produce

```
USS 8649 275 Asia
Can 3852 25 North America
Chi 3705 1032 Asia
USA 3615 237 North America
Bra 3286 134 South America
Ind 1267 746 Asia
Mex 762 78 North America
Fra 211 55 Europe
Jap 144 120 Asia
Ger 96 61 Europe
Eng 94 56 Europe
```

Setting $1 forces awk to recompute $0 and thus the fields are now separated by a blank (the default value of OFS), no longer by a tab.

Strings are concatenated merely by writing them one after another in an expression. For example, on the countries file,

```
      { s = s substr($1, 1, 3) " " }
   END { print s }
```

prints

```
   USS Can Chi USA Bra Ind Mex Fra Jap Ger Eng
```

by building `s` up a piece at a time starting with an initially empty string. (If you are worried about the extra blank on the end, use

```
   print substr(s, 1, length(s)-1)
```

instead of `print s` in the END action.)

Number or String? The value of an expression may be automatically converted from a number to a string or vice versa, depending on what operation is applied to it. In an arithmetic expression like

```
   pop + $3
```

the operands `pop` and `$3` must be numeric, so their values will be forced or *coerced* to numbers if they are not already. Similarly, in the assignment expression

```
   pop += $3
```

`pop` and `$3` must be numbers. In a string expression like

```
   $1 $2
```

the operands `$1` and `$2` must be strings to be concatenated, so they will be coerced to strings if necessary.

In contexts where the same operator applies to both numbers and strings, there are special rules. In the assignment $v = e$, both the assignment and the variable v acquire the type of the expression e. In a comparison expression like

```
   x == y
```

if both operands have a numeric type, the comparison is numeric; otherwise, any numeric operand is coerced to a string and the comparison is made on the string values.

Let us examine what this rule means for a comparison like

```
   $1 == $2
```

that involves fields. Here, the type of the comparison depends on whether the fields contain numbers or strings, and this can only be determined when the program runs; the type of the comparison may differ from input line to input line. When awk creates a field at run time, it automatically sets its type to string; in addition, if the field contains a machine-representable number, it also gives the field a numeric type.

For example, the comparison `$1 == $2` will be numeric and succeed if `$1` and `$2` have any of the values

```
1    1.0    +1    1e0    0.1e+1    10E-1    001
```

because all these values are different representations of the number 1. However, this same expression will be a string comparison and hence fail on each of these pairs:

```
0          (null)
0.0        (null)
0          0a
1e500      1.0e500
```

In the first three pairs, the second field is not a number. The last pair will be compared as strings on machines where the values are too large to be represented as numbers.

The print statement

```
print $1
```

prints the string value of the first field; thus, the output is identical to the input.

Uninitialized variables are created with the numeric value 0 and the string value "". Nonexistent fields and fields that are explicitly null have only the string value ""; they are not numeric, but when coerced to numbers they acquire the numeric value 0. As we will see at the end of this section, array subscripts are strings.

There are two idioms for coercing an expression of one type to the other:

> *number* ""   concatenate a null string to *number* to coerce it to a string
> *string* + 0   add zero to *string* to coerce it to a number

Thus, to force a string comparison between two fields, coerce one field to string:

```
$1 "" == $2
```

To force a numeric comparison, coerce *both* fields to numeric:

```
$1 + 0 == $2 + 0
```

This works regardless of what the fields contain.

The numeric value of a string is the value of the longest prefix of the string that looks numeric. Thus

```
BEGIN { print "1E2"+0, "12E"+0, "E12"+0, "1X2Y3"+0 }
```

yields

```
100 12 0 1
```

The string value of a number is computed by formatting the number with the output format conversion OFMT. OFMT also controls the conversion of numeric values to strings for concatenation, comparison, and creation of array subscripts. The default value of OFMT is "%.6g". Thus

```
BEGIN { print 1E2 "", 12E-2 "", E12 "", 1.23456789 "" }
```

gives

```
100 0.12  1.23457
```

The default value of OFMT can be changed by assigning it a new value. If OFMT were changed to "%.2f", for example, numbers would be printed, and coerced numbers would be compared, with two digits after the decimal point.

TABLE 2-8. EXPRESSION OPERATORS

OPERATION	OPERATORS	EXAMPLE	MEANING OF EXAMPLE
assignment	= += -= *= /= %= ^=	x *= 2	x = x * 2
conditional	?:	x?y:z	if x is true then y else z
logical OR	¦¦	x ¦¦ y	1 if x or y is true, 0 otherwise
logical AND	&&	x && y	1 if x and y are true, 0 otherwise
array membership	in	i in a	1 if a[i] exists, 0 otherwise
matching	~ !~	$1 ~ /x/	1 if the first field contains an x, 0 otherwise
relational	< <= == != >= >	x == y	1 if x is equal to y, 0 otherwise
concatenation		"a" "bc"	"abc"; there is no explicit concatenation operator
add, subtract	+ -	x + y	sum of x and y
multiply, divide, mod	* / %	x % y	remainder of x divided by y
unary plus and minus	+ -	-x	negated value of x
logical NOT	!	!$1	1 if $1 is zero or null, 0 otherwise
exponentiation	^	x ^ y	x^y
increment, decrement	++ --	++x, x++	add 1 to x
field	$	$i+1	value of i-th field, plus 1
grouping	( )	($i)++	add 1 to value of i-th field

Summary of Operators. The operators that can appear in expressions are summarized in Table 2-8. Expressions can be created by applying these operators to constants, variables, field names, array elements, functions, and other expressions.

The operators are listed in order of increasing precedence. Operators of higher precedence are evaluated before lower ones; this means, for example, that * is evaluated before + in an expression. All operators are left associative except the assignment operators, the conditional operator, and exponentiation, which are right associative. Left associativity means that operators of the same precedence are evaluated left to right; thus 3-2-1 is (3-2)-1, not 3-(2-1).

Since there is no explicit operator for concatenation, it is wise to parenthesize expressions involving other operators in concatenations. Consider the program

```
$1 < 0 { print "abs($1) = " -$1 }
```

The expression following print seems to use concatenation, but is actually a subtraction. The programs

```
$1 < 0 { print "abs($1) = " (-$1) }
```

and

```
$1 < 0 { print "abs($1) =", -$1 }
```

both do what was intended.

Control-Flow Statements

Awk provides braces for grouping statements, an if-else statement for decision-making, and while, for, and do statements for looping. All of these statements were adopted from C.

A single statement can always be replaced by a list of statements enclosed in braces. The statements in the list are separated by newlines or semicolons. Newlines may be put after any left brace and before any right brace.

The if-else statement has the form

```
if (expression)
    statement₁
else
    statement₂
```

The else *statement₂* is optional. Newlines are optional after the right parenthesis, after *statement₁*, and after the keyword else. If else appears on the same line as *statement₁*, then a semicolon must terminate *statement₁* if it is a single statement.

In an if-else statement, the test *expression* is evaluated first. If it is true, that is, either nonzero or nonnull, *statement₁* is executed. If *expression* is false, that is, either zero or null, and else *statement₂* is present, then *statement₂* is executed.

To eliminate any ambiguity, we adopt the rule that each else is associated with the closest previous unassociated if. For example, the else in the statement

```
if (e1) if (e2) s=1; else s=2
```

is associated with the second if. (The semicolon after s=1 is required, since the else appears on the same line.)

The while statement repeatedly executes a statement while a condition is true:

Control-Flow Statements

{ *statements* }
    statement grouping
if (*expression*) *statement*
    if *expression* is true, execute *statement*
if (*expression*) *statement*₁ else *statement*₂
    if *expression* is true, execute *statement*₁ otherwise execute *statement*₂
while (*expression*) *statement*
    if *expression* is true, execute *statement*, then repeat
for (*expression*₁ ; *expression*₂ ; *expression*₃) *statement*
    equivalent to *expression*₁ ; while (*expression*₂) { *statement*; *expression*₃ }
for (*variable* in *array*) *statement*
    execute *statement* with *variable* set to each subscript in *array* in turn
do *statement* while (*expression*)
    execute *statement*; if *expression* is true, repeat
break
    immediately leave innermost enclosing while, for or do
continue
    start next iteration of innermost enclosing while, for or do
next
    start next iteration of main input loop
exit
exit *expression*
    go immediately to the END action; if within the END action, exit program entirely.
    Return *expression* as program status.

```
while (expression)
    statement
```

Newlines are optional after the right parenthesis. In this loop, *expression* is evaluated; if it is true, *statement* is executed and *expression* is tested again. The cycle repeats as long as *expression* is true. For example, this program prints all input fields, one per line:

```
{    i = 1
     while (i <= NF) {
          print $i
          i++
     }
}
```

The loop stops when i reaches NF+1, and that is its value after the loop exits.

The for statement is a more general form of while:

```
for (expression₁; expression₂; expression₃)
    statement
```

Newlines are optional after the right parenthesis. The `for` statement has the same effect as

```
expression₁
while (expression₂) {
    statement
    expression₃
}
```

so

```
{ for (i = 1; i <= NF; i++)
      print $i
}
```

does the same loop over the fields as the `while` example above. In the `for` statement, all three expressions are optional. If *expression₂* is missing, the condition is taken to be always true, so `for( ; ; )` is an infinite loop.

An alternate version of the `for` statement that loops over array subscripts is described in the section on arrays.

The `do` statement has the form

```
do
    statement
while (expression)
```

Newlines are optional after the keyword `do` and after *statement*. If `while` appears on the same line as *statement*, then *statement* must be terminated by a semicolon if it is a single statement. The `do` loop executes *statement* once, then repeats *statement* as long as *expression* is true. It differs from the `while` and `for` in a critical way: its test for completion is at the bottom instead of the top, so it always goes through the loop at least once.

There are two statements for modifying how loops cycle: `break` and `continue`. The `break` statement causes an exit from the immediately enclosing `while` or `for` or `do`. The `continue` statement causes the next iteration to begin; it causes execution to go to the test expression in the `while` and `do`, and to *expression₃* in the `for` statement.

The `next` and `exit` statements control the outer loop that reads the input lines in an awk program. The `next` statement causes awk to fetch the next input line and begin matching patterns starting from the first pattern-action statement. In an `END` action, the `exit` statement causes the program to terminate. In any other action, it causes the program to behave as if the end of the input had occurred; no more input is read, and the `END` actions, if any, are executed.

If an `exit` statement contains an expression

```
exit expr
```

it causes awk to return the value of *expr* as its exit status unless overridden by a subsequent error or `exit`. If there is no *expr*, the exit status is zero. In some operating systems, including Unix, the exit status may be tested by the program that invoked awk.

Empty Statement

A semicolon by itself denotes the empty statement. In the following program, the body of the `for` loop is an empty statement.

```
BEGIN { FS = "\t" }
      { for (i = 1; i <= NF && $i != ""; i++)
          ;
        if (i <= NF)
            print
      }
```

The program prints all lines that contain an empty field.

Arrays

Awk provides one-dimensional arrays for storing strings and numbers. Arrays and array elements need not be declared, nor is there any need to specify how many elements an array has. Like variables, array elements spring into existence by being mentioned; at birth, they have the numeric value 0 and the string value `""`.

As a simple example, the statement

```
x[NR] = $0
```

assigns the current input line to element `NR` of the array `x`. In fact, it is easy (though perhaps slow) to read the entire input into an array, then process it in any convenient order. For example, this variant of the program from Section 1.7 prints its input in reverse line order:

```
    { x[NR] = $0 }
END { for (i = NR; i > 0; i--) print x[i] }
```

The first action merely records each input line in the array `x`, using the line number as a subscript; the real work is done in the `END` statement.

The characteristic that sets awk arrays apart from those in most other languages is that subscripts are strings. This gives awk a capability like the associative memory of SNOBOL4 tables, and for this reason, arrays in awk are called *associative arrays*.

The following program accumulates the populations of `Asia` and `Europe` in the array `pop`. The `END` action prints the total populations of these two continents.

```
/Asia/    { pop["Asia"] += $3 }
/Europe/  { pop["Europe"] += $3 }
END       { print "Asian population is",
                   pop["Asia"], "million."
            print "European population is",
                   pop["Europe"], "million."
          }
```

On countries, this program generates

```
Asian population is 2173 million.
European population is 172 million.
```

Note that the subscripts are the string constants "Asia" and "Europe". If we had written pop[Asia] instead of pop["Asia"], the expression would have used the value of the variable Asia as the subscript, and since the variable is uninitialized, the values would have been accumulated in pop[""].

This example doesn't really need an associative array since there are only two elements, both named explicitly. Suppose instead that our task is to determine the total population for each continent. Associative arrays are ideally suited for this kind of aggregation. Any expression can be used as a subscript in an array reference, so

```
pop[$4] += $3
```

uses the string in the fourth field of the current input line to index the array pop and in that entry accumulates the value of the third field:

```
BEGIN { FS = "\t" }
      { pop[$4] += $3 }
END   { for (name in pop)
            print name, pop[name]
      }
```

The subscripts of the array pop are the continent names; the values are the accumulated populations. This code works regardless of the number of continents; the output from the countries file is

```
North America 340
South America 134
Asia 2173
Europe 172
```

The last program used a form of the for statement that loops over all subscripts of an array:

```
for (variable in array)
    statement
```

This loop executes *statement* with *variable* set in turn to each different subscript in the array. The order in which the subscripts are considered is implementation dependent. Results are unpredictable if new elements are added to the array by *statement*.

You can determine whether a particular subscript occurs in an array with the expression

> *subscript* in *A*

This expression has the value 1 if *A* [*subscript*] already exists, and 0 otherwise. Thus, to test whether `Africa` is a subscript of the array `pop` you can say

```
if ("Africa" in pop) ...
```

This condition performs the test without the side effect of creating `pop["Africa"]`, which would happen if you used

```
if (pop["Africa"] != "") ...
```

Note that neither is a test of whether the array `pop` contains an element with value `"Africa"`.

The `delete` Statement. An array element may be deleted with

> delete *array*[*subscript*]

For example, this loop removes all the elements from the array `pop`:

```
for (i in pop)
    delete pop[i]
```

The `split` Function. The function `split(`*str*`,`*arr*`,`*fs*`)` splits the string value of *str* into fields and stores them in the array *arr*. The number of fields produced is returned as the value of `split`. The string value of the third argument, *fs*, determines the field separator. If there is no third argument, `FS` is used. In either case, the rules are as for input field splitting, which is discussed in Section 2.5. The function

```
split("7/4/76", arr, "/")
```

splits the string `7/4/76` into three fields using `/` as the separator; it stores 7 in `arr["1"]`, 4 in `arr["2"]`, and 76 in `arr["3"]`.

Strings are versatile array subscripts, but the behavior of numeric subscripts as strings may sometimes appear counterintuitive. Since the string values of 1 and `"1"` are the same, `arr[1]` is the same as `arr["1"]`. But notice that 0 1 is not the same string as 1 and the string 10 comes before the string 2.

Multidimensional Arrays. Awk does not support multidimensional arrays directly but it provides a simulation using one-dimensional arrays. Although you can write multidimensional subscripts like `i,j` or `s,p,q,r`, awk concatenates the components of the subscripts (with a separator between them) to synthesize a single subscript out of the multiple subscripts you write. For example,

```
for (i = 1; i <= 10; i++)
    for (j = 1; j <= 10; j++)
        arr[i, j] = 0
```

creates an array of 100 elements whose subscripts appear to have the form 1, 1, 1, 2, and so on. Internally, however, these subscripts are stored as strings of the form 1 SUBSEP 1, 1 SUBSEP 2, and so on. The built-in variable SUBSEP contains the value of the subscript-component separator; its default value is not a comma but "\034", a value that is unlikely to appear in normal text.

The test for array membership with multidimensional subscripts uses a parenthesized list of subscripts, such as

```
if ((i,j) in arr) ...
```

To loop over such an array, however, you would write

```
for (k in arr) ...
```

and use split(k,x,SUBSEP) if access to the individual subscript components is needed.

Array elements cannot themselves be arrays.

2.3   User-Defined Functions

In addition to built-in functions, an awk program can contain user-defined functions. Such a function is defined by a statement of the form

```
function name(parameter-list) {
    statements
}
```

A function definition can occur anywhere a pattern-action statement can. Thus, the general form of an awk program is a sequence of pattern-action statements and function definitions separated by newlines or semicolons.

In a function definition, newlines are optional after the left brace and before the right brace of the function body. The parameter list is a sequence of variable names separated by commas; within the body of the function these variables refer to the arguments with which the function was called.

The body of a function definition may contain a return statement that returns control and perhaps a value to the caller. It has the form

```
return expression
```

The expression is optional, and so is the return statement itself, but the returned value is undefined if none is provided or if the last statement executed is not a return.

For example, this function computes the maximum of its arguments:

```
function max(m, n) {
    return m > n ? m : n
}
```

The variables m and n belong to the function max; they are unrelated to any other variables of the same names elsewhere in the program.

A user-defined function can be used in any expression in any pattern-action statement or the body of any function definition. Each use is a *call* of the function. If a user-defined function is called in the body of its own definition, that function is said to be *recursive*.

For example, the max function might be called like this:

```
{ print max($1,max($2,$3)) }   # print maximum of $1, $2, $3

function max(m, n) {
    return m > n ? m : n
}
```

There cannot be any blanks between the function name and the left parenthesis of the argument list when the function is called.

When a function is called with an argument like $1, which is just an ordinary variable, the function is given a copy of the value of the variable, so the function manipulates the copy, not the variable itself. This means that the function cannot affect the value of the variable outside the function. (The jargon is that such variables, called "scalars," are passed "by value.") Arrays are not copied, however, so it is possible for the function to alter array elements or create new ones. (This is called passing "by reference.") The name of a function may not be used as a parameter.

To repeat, within a function definition, the parameters are local variables — they last only as long as the function is executing, and they are unrelated to variables of the same name elsewhere in the program. But *all other variables are global*; if a variable is not named in the parameter list, it is visible and accessible throughout the program.

This means that the way to provide local variables for the private use of a function is to include them at the end of the parameter list in the function definition. Any variable in the parameter list for which no actual parameter is supplied in a call is a local variable, with null initial value. This is not a very elegant language design but it at least provides the necessary facility. We put several blanks between the arguments and the local variables so they can be distinguished.

2.4   Output

The print and printf statements generate output. The print statement is used for simple output; printf is used when careful formatting is required. Output from print and printf can be directed into files and pipes as well as to the terminal. These statements can be used in any mixture; the output comes out in the order in which it is generated.

Output Statements

```
print
```
    print $0 on standard output
`print` *expression*, *expression*, ...
    print *expression*'s, separated by OFS, terminated by ORS
`print` *expression*, *expression*, ... >*filename*
    print on file *filename* instead of standard output
`print` *expression*, *expression*, ... >>*filename*
    append to file *filename* instead of overwriting previous contents
`print` *expression*, *expression*, ... ¦ *command*
    print to standard input of *command*
`printf`(*format*, *expression*, *expression*, ...)
`printf`(*format*, *expression*, *expression*, ...) >*filename*
`printf`(*format*, *expression*, *expression*, ...) >>*filename*
`printf`(*format*, *expression*, *expression*, ...) ¦ *command*
    printf statements are like print but the first argument specifies output format
`close`(*filename*), `close`(*command*)
    break connection between print and *filename* or *command*
`system`(*command*)
    execute *command*; value is status return of *command*

The argument list of a `printf` statement does not need to be enclosed in parentheses. But if an expression in the argument list of a `print` or `printf` statement contains a relational operator, either the expression or the argument list must be enclosed in parentheses. Pipes and `system` may not be available on non-Unix systems.

The `print` Statement

The `print` statement has two forms:

$$\text{print } expr_1, \; expr_2, \; \dots \; , \; expr_n$$
$$\text{print}(expr_1, \; expr_2, \; \dots \; , \; expr_n)$$

Both forms print the string value of each expression separated by the output field separator followed by the output record separator. The statement

    print

is an abbreviation for

    print $0

To print a blank line, that is, a line with only a newline, use

    print ""

The second form of the `print` statement encloses the argument list in parentheses, as in

```
print($1 ":", $2)
```

Both forms of the print statement generate the same output but, as we will see, parentheses are necessary for arguments containing relational operators.

Output Separators

The output field separator and output record separator are stored in the built-in variables OFS and ORS. Initially, OFS is set to a single blank and ORS to a single newline, but these values can be changed at any time. For example, the following program prints the first and second fields of each line with a colon between the fields and two newlines after the second field:

```
BEGIN    { OFS = ":"; ORS = "\n\n" }
         { print $1, $2 }
```

By contrast,

```
         { print $1 $2 }
```

prints the first and second fields with no intervening output field separator, because $1 $2 is a string consisting of the concatenation of the two fields.

The printf Statement

The printf statement is used to generate formatted output. It is similar to that in C except that the * format specifier is not supported. Like print, it has both an unparenthesized and parenthesized form:

```
printf format, expr₁, expr₂, ... , exprₙ
printf(format, expr₁, expr₂, ... , exprₙ)
```

The *format* argument is always required; it is an expression whose string value contains both literal text to be printed and specifications of how the expressions in the argument list are to be formatted, as in Table 2-9. Each specification begins with a %, ends with a character that determines the conversion, and may include three modifiers:

-	left-justify expression in its field
width	pad field to this width as needed; leading 0 pads with zeros
.*prec*	maximum string width, or digits to right of decimal point

Table 2-10 contains some examples of specifications, data, and the corresponding output. Output produced by printf does not contain any newlines unless you put them in explicitly.

Output into Files

The redirection operators > and >> are used to put output into files instead of the standard output. The following program will put the first and third fields of all input lines into two files: bigpop if the third field is greater than 100,

TABLE 2-9. PRINTF FORMAT-CONTROL CHARACTERS

CHARACTER	PRINT EXPRESSION AS
c	ASCII character
d	decimal integer
e	[-]d.ddddddE[+-]dd
f	[-]ddd.dddddd
g	e or f conversion, whichever is shorter, with nonsignificant zeros suppressed
o	unsigned octal number
s	string
x	unsigned hexadecimal number
%	print a %; no argument is consumed

TABLE 2-10. EXAMPLES OF PRINTF SPECIFICATIONS

fmt	$1	printf(fmt, $1)
%c	97	a
%d	97.5	97
%5d	97.5	97
%e	97.5	9.750000e+01
%f	97.5	97.500000
%7.2f	97.5	97.50
%g	97.5	97.5
%.6g	97.5	97.5
%o	97	141
%06o	97	000141
%x	97	61
¦%s¦	January	¦January¦
¦%10s¦	January	¦ January¦
¦%-10s¦	January	¦January ¦
¦%.3s¦	January	¦Jan¦
¦%10.3s¦	January	¦ Jan¦
¦%-10.3s¦	January	¦Jan ¦
%%	January	%

and `smallpop` otherwise:

```
$3 > 100    { print $1, $3 >"bigpop" }
$3 <= 100   { print $1, $3 >"smallpop" }
```

Notice that the filenames have to be quoted; without quotes, `bigpop` and `smallpop` are merely uninitialized variables. Filenames can be variables or expressions as well:

```
{ print($1, $3) > ($3 > 100 ? "bigpop" : "smallpop") }
```

does the same job, and the program

```
{ print > $1 }
```

puts every input line into a file named by the first field.

In `print` and `printf` statements, if an expression in the argument list contains a relational operator, then either that expression or the argument list needs to be parenthesized. This rule eliminates any potential ambiguity arising from the redirection operator >. In

```
{ print $1, $2 > $3 }
```

> is the redirection operator, and hence not part of the second expression, so the values of the first two fields are written to the file named in the third field. If you want the second expression to include the > operator, use parentheses:

```
{ print $1, ($2 > $3) }
```

It is also important to note that a redirection operator opens a file only once; each successive `print` or `printf` statement adds more data to the open file. When the redirection operator > is used, the file is initially cleared before any output is written to it. If >> is used instead of >, the file is not initially cleared; output is appended after the original contents.

Output into Pipes

It is also possible to direct output into a pipe instead of a file on systems that support pipes. The statement

```
print | command
```

causes the output of `print` to be piped into the *command*.

Suppose we want to create a list of continent-population pairs, sorted in reverse numeric order by population. The program below accumulates in an array pop the population values in the third field for each of the distinct continent names in the fourth field. The END action prints each continent name and its population, and pipes this output into a suitable `sort` command.

```
# print continents and populations, sorted by population

BEGIN { FS = "\t" }
      { pop[$4] += $3 }
END   { for (c in pop)
            printf("%15s\t%6d\n", c, pop[c]) | "sort -t'\t' +1rn"
      }
```

This yields

```
        Asia       2173
North America        340
      Europe        172
South America        134
```

Another use for a pipe is writing onto the standard error file on Unix systems; output written there appears on the user's terminal instead of the standard output. There are several idioms for writing on the standard error file:

```
print message ¦ "cat 1>&2"           # redirect cat to stderr
system("echo '" message "' 1>&2")    # redirect echo to stderr
print message > "/dev/tty"           # write directly on terminal
```

Although most of our examples show literal strings enclosed in quotes, command lines and filenames can be specified by any expression. In print statements involving redirection of output, the files or pipes are identified by their names; that is, the pipe in the program above is literally named

```
sort -t'\t' +1rn
```

Normally, a file or pipe is created and opened only once during the run of a program. If the file or pipe is explicitly closed and then reused, it will be reopened.

Closing Files and Pipes

The statement close(*expr*) closes a file or pipe denoted by *expr*; the string value of *expr* must be the same as the string used to create the file or pipe in the first place. Thus

```
close("sort -t'\t' +1rn")
```

closes the sort pipe opened above.

close is necessary if you intend to write a file, then read it later in the same program. There are also system-defined limits on the number of files and pipes that can be open at the same time.

2.5 Input

There are several ways of providing input to an awk program. The most common arrangement is to put input data in a file, say data, and then type

```
awk 'program' data
```

Awk reads its standard input if no filenames are given; thus, a second common arrangement is to have another program pipe its output into awk. For example, the program egrep selects input lines containing a specified regular expression, but it does this much faster than awk does. We could therefore type the command

```
egrep 'Asia' countries ¦ awk 'program'
```

egrep finds the lines containing Asia and passes them on to the awk program for subsequent processing.

Input Separators

The default value of the built-in variable FS is " ", that is, a single blank. When FS has this specific value, input fields are separated by blanks and/or tabs, and leading blanks and tabs are discarded, so each of the following lines has the same first field:

```
field1
  field1
    field1        field2
```

When FS has any other value, however, leading blanks and tabs are *not* discarded.

The field separator can be changed by assigning a string to the built-in variable FS. If the string is longer than one character, it is taken to be a regular expression. The leftmost longest nonnull and nonoverlapping substrings matched by that regular expression become the field separators in the current input line. For example,

```
BEGIN { FS = ",[ \t]*¦[ \t]+" }
```

makes every string consisting of a comma followed by blanks and tabs, and every string of blanks and tabs without a comma, into field separators.

When FS is set to a single character other than blank, that character becomes the field separator. This convention makes it easy to use regular expression metacharacters as field separators:

```
FS = "¦"
```

makes ¦ a field separator. But note that something indirect like

```
FS = "[ ]"
```

is required to set the field separator to a single blank.

FS can also be set on the command line with the -F argument. The command line

```
awk -F',[ \t]*¦[ \t]+' 'program'
```

sets the field separator to the same strings as the BEGIN action shown above.

Multiline Records

By default, records are separated by newlines, so the terms "line" and "record" are normally synonymous. The default record separator can be changed in a limited way, however, by assigning a new value to the built-in record-separator variable RS. If RS is set to the null string, as in

```
BEGIN   { RS = "" }
```

then records are separated by one or more blank lines and each record can therefore occupy several lines. Setting RS back to newline with the assignment RS = "\n" restores the default behavior. With multiline records, no matter what value FS has, newline is always one of the field separators.

A common way to process multiline records is to use

```
BEGIN   { RS = ""; FS = "\n" }
```

to set the record separator to one or more blank lines and the field separator to a newline alone; each line is thus a separate field. There is a limit on how long a record can be, usually about 3000 characters. Chapter 3 contains more discussion of how to handle multiline records.

The getline Function

The function getline can be used to read input either from the current input or from a file or pipe. By itself, getline fetches the next input record and performs the normal field-splitting operations on it. It sets NF, NR, and FNR; it returns 1 if there was a record present, 0 if end-of-file was encountered, and −1 if some error occurred (such as failure to open a file).

The expression getline x reads the next record into the variable x and increments NR and FNR. No splitting is done; NF is not set.

The expression

```
getline <"file"
```

reads from file instead of the current input. It has no effect on NR or FNR, but field splitting is performed and NF is set.

The expression

```
getline x <"file"
```

gets the next record from file into x; no splitting is done, and NF, NR, and FNR are untouched.

Table 2-11 summarizes the forms of the getline function. The value of each expression is the value returned by getline.

As an example, this program copies its input to its output, except that each line like

```
#include "filename"
```

is replaced by the contents of the file filename.

TABLE 2-11. GETLINE FUNCTION

EXPRESSION	SETS
getline	$0, NF, NR, FNR
getline *var*	*var*, NR, FNR
getline <*file*	$0, NF
getline *var* <*file*	*var*
cmd ¦ getline	$0, NF
cmd ¦ getline *var*	*var*

```
# include - replace #include "f" by contents of file f

/^#include/ {
    gsub(/"/, "", $2)
    while (getline x <$2 > 0)
        print x
    next
}
{ print }
```

It is also possible to pipe the output of another command directly into getline. For example, the statement

```
while ("who" ¦ getline)
    n++
```

executes the Unix program who (once only) and pipes its output into getline. The output of who is a list of the users logged in. Each iteration of the while loop reads one more line from this list and increments the variable n, so after the while loop terminates, n contains a count of the number of users. Similarly, the expression

```
"date" ¦ getline d
```

pipes the output of the date command into the variable d, thus setting d to the current date. Again, input pipes may not be available on non-Unix systems.

In all cases involving getline, you should be aware of the possibility of an error return if the file can't be accessed. Although it's appealing to write

```
while (getline <"file") ...      # Dangerous
```

that's an infinite loop if file doesn't exist, because with a nonexistent file getline returns −1, a nonzero value that represents true. The preferred way is

```
while (getline <"file" > 0) ... # Safe
```

Here the loop will be executed only when getline returns 1.

Command-Line Variable Assignments

As we have seen, an awk command line can have several forms:

```
awk 'program' f1 f2 ...
awk -f progfile f1 f2 ...
awk -Fsep 'program' f1 f2 ...
awk -Fsep -f progfile f1 f2 ...
```

In these command lines, f1, f2, etc., are command-line arguments that normally represent filenames. If a filename has the form *var=text*, however, it is
treated as an assignment of *text* to *var*, performed at the time when that argument would otherwise be accessed as a file. This type of assignment allows variables to be changed before and after a file is read.

Command-Line Arguments

The command-line arguments are available to the awk program in a built-in
array called ARGV. The value of the built-in variable ARGC is one more than
the number of arguments. With the command line

```
awk -f progfile a v=1 b
```

ARGC has the value 4, ARGV[0] contains awk, ARGV[1] contains a, ARGV[2]
contains v=1, and ARGV[3] contains b. ARGC is one more than the number of
arguments because awk, the name of the command, is counted as argument
zero, as it is in C programs. If the awk program appears on the command line,
however, the program is not treated as an argument, nor is -f *filename* or any
-F option. For example, with the command line

```
awk -F'\t' '$3 > 100' countries
```

ARGC is 2 and ARGV[1] is countries.

The following program echoes its command-line arguments:

```
# echo - print command-line arguments

BEGIN {
    for (i = 1; i < ARGC; i++)
        printf "%s ", ARGV[i]
    printf "\n"
}
```

Notice that everything happens in the BEGIN action: because there are no other
pattern-action statements, the arguments are never treated as filenames, and no
input is read.

Another program using command-line arguments is seq, which generates
sequences of integers:

```
# seq - print sequences of integers
#    input:  arguments q, p q, or p q r;   q >= p; r > 0
#    output: integers 1 to q, p to q, or p to q in steps of r

BEGIN {
    if (ARGC == 2)
        for (i = 1; i <= ARGV[1]; i++)
            print i
    else if (ARGC == 3)
        for (i = ARGV[1]; i <= ARGV[2]; i++)
            print i
    else if (ARGC == 4)
        for (i = ARGV[1]; i <= ARGV[2]; i += ARGV[3])
            print i
}
```

The commands

```
awk -f seq 10
awk -f seq 1 10
awk -f seq 1 10 1
```

all generate the integers one through ten.

The arguments in ARGV may be modified or added to; ARGC may be altered. As each input file ends, awk treats the next nonnull element of ARGV (up through the current value of ARGC-1) as the name of the next input file. Thus setting an element of ARGV to null means that it will not be treated as an input file. The name "-" may be used for the standard input.

2.6   Interaction with Other Programs

This section describes some of the ways in which awk programs can cooperate with other commands. The discussion applies primarily to the Unix operating system; the examples here may fail or work differently on non-Unix systems.

The system Function

The built-in function system(*expression*) executes the command given by the string value of *expression*. The value returned by system is the status returned by the command executed.

For example, we can build another version of the file-inclusion program of Section 2.5 like this:

```
$1 == "#include" { gsub(/"/, "", $2); system("cat " $2); next }
                 { print }
```

If the first field is #include, quotes are removed, and the Unix command cat is called to print the file named in the second field. Other lines are just copied.

Making a Shell Command from an AWK Program

In all of the examples so far, the awk program was in a file and fetched with the -f flag, or it appeared on the command line enclosed in single quotes, like this:

```
awk '{ print $1 }' ...
```

Since awk uses many of the same characters as the shell does, such as $ and ", surrounding the program with single quotes ensures that the shell will pass the entire program unchanged to awk.

Both methods of invoking the awk program require some typing. To reduce the number of keystrokes, we might want to put both the command and the program into an executable file, and invoke the command by typing just the name of the file. Suppose we want to create a command field1 that will print the first field of each line of input. This is easy: we put

```
awk '{print $1}' $*
```

into the file field1, and make the file executable by typing the Unix command

```
chmod +x field1
```

We can now print the first field of each line of a set of files by typing

```
field1 filenames ...
```

Now, consider writing a more general command field that will print an arbitrary combination of fields from each line of its input; in other words, the command

```
field n₁ n₂ ... file₁ file₂ ...
```

will print the specified fields in the specified order. How do we get the value of each n_i into the awk program each time it is run and how do we distinguish the n_i's from the filename arguments?

There are several ways to do this if one is adept in shell programming. The simplest way that uses only awk, however, is to scan through the built-in array ARGV to process the n_i's, resetting each such argument to the null string so that it is not treated as a filename.

```
# field - print named fields of each input line
#    usage:  field n n n ... file file file ...

awk '
BEGIN {
    for (i = 1; ARGV[i] ~ /^[0-9]+$/; i++) { # collect numbers
        fld[++nf] = ARGV[i]
        ARGV[i] = ""
    }
    if (i >= ARGC)   # no file names so force stdin
        ARGV[ARGC++] = "-"
}
{   for (i = 1; i <= nf; i++)
        printf("%s%s", $fld[i], i < nf ? " " : "\n")
}
' $*
```

This version can deal with either standard input or a list of filename arguments, and with any number of fields in any order.

2.7 Summary

As we said earlier, this is a long chapter, packed with details, and you are dedicated indeed if you have read every word to get here. You will find that it pays to go back and re-read sections from time to time, either to see precisely how something works, or because one of the examples in later chapters suggests a construction that you might not have tried before.

Awk, like any language, is best learned by experience and practice, so we encourage you to go off and write your own programs. They don't have to be big or complicated — you can usually learn how some feature works or test some crucial point with only a couple of lines of code, and you can just type in data to see how the program behaves.

Bibliographic Notes

The programming language C is described in *The C Programming Language*, by Brian Kernighan and Dennis Ritchie (Prentice-Hall, 1978). There are numerous books on how to use the Unix system; *The Unix Programming Environment*, by Brian Kernighan and Rob Pike (Prentice-Hall, 1984) has an extensive discussion of how to create shell programs that include awk.

3 DATA PROCESSING

Awk was originally intended for everyday data-processing tasks, such as information retrieval, data validation, and data transformation and reduction. We have already seen simple examples of these in Chapters 1 and 2. In this chapter, we will consider more complex tasks of a similar nature. Most of the examples deal with the usual line-at-a-time processing, but the final section describes how to handle data where an input record may occupy several lines.

Awk programs are often developed incrementally: a few lines are written and tested, then a few more added, and so on. Many of the longer programs in this book were developed in this way.

It's also possible to write awk programs in the traditional way, sketching the outline of the program, consulting the language manual, and so forth. But modifying an existing program to get the desired effect is frequently easier. The programs in this book thus serve another purpose, providing useful models for programming by example.

3.1 Data Transformation and Reduction

One of the most common uses of awk is to transform data from one form to another, usually from the form produced by one program to a different form required by some other program. Another use is selection of relevant data from a larger data set, often with reformatting and the preparation of summary information. This section contains a variety of examples of these topics.

Summing Columns

We have already seen several variants of the two-line awk program that adds up all the numbers in a single field. The following program performs a somewhat more complicated but still representative data-reduction task. Every input line has several fields, each containing numbers, and the task is to compute the sum of each column of numbers, regardless of how many columns there are.

```
# sum1 - print column sums
#    input:  rows of numbers
#    output: sum of each column
#       missing entries are treated as zeros

    { for (i = 1; i <= NF; i++)
          sum[i] += $i
      if (NF > maxfld)
          maxfld = NF
    }
END { for (i = 1; i <= maxfld; i++) {
          printf("%g", sum[i])
          if (i < maxfld)
              printf("\t")
          else
              printf("\n")
    }
  }
```

Automatic initialization is convenient here since maxfld, the largest number of fields seen so far in any row, starts off at zero automatically, as do all of the entries in the sum array, even though it's not known until the end how many there are. It's also worth noting that the program prints nothing if the input file is empty.

It's convenient that the program doesn't need to be told how many fields a row has, but it doesn't check that the entries are all numbers, nor that each row has the same number of entries. The following program does the same job, but also checks that each row has the same number of entries as the first:

```
# sum2 - print column sums
#      check that each line has the same number of fields
#           as line one

NR==1 { nfld = NF }
      { for (i = 1; i <= NF; i++)
            sum[i] += $i
        if (NF != nfld)
            print "line " NR " has " NF " entries, not " nfld
      }
END   { for (i = 1; i <= nfld; i++)
            printf("%g%s", sum[i], i < nfld ? "\t" : "\n")
      }
```

We also revised the output code in the END action, to show how a conditional expression can be used to put tabs between the column sums and a newline after the last sum.

Now suppose that some of the fields are nonnumeric, so they shouldn't be included in the sums. The strategy is to add an array numcol to keep track of which fields are numeric, and a function isnum to check if an entry is a number. This is made a function so the test is only in one place, in anticipation of future changes. If the program can trust its input, it need only look at the first line to tell if a field will be numeric. The variable nfld is needed because NF is zero inside the END action.

```
# sum3 - print sums of numeric columns
#      input:  rows of integers and strings
#      output: sums of numeric columns
#         assumes every line has same layout

NR==1 { nfld = NF
        for (i = 1; i <= NF; i++)
            numcol[i] = isnum($i)
      }

      { for (i = 1; i <= NF; i++)
            if (numcol[i])
                sum[i] += $i
      }

END   { for (i = 1; i <= nfld; i++) {
            if (numcol[i])
                printf("%g", sum[i])
            else
                printf("--")
            printf(i < nfld ? "\t" : "\n")
          }
      }

function isnum(n) { return n ~ /^[+-]?[0-9]+$/ }
```

The function isnum defines a number as one or more digits, perhaps preceded by a sign. A more general definition for numbers can be found in the discussion of regular expressions in Section 2.1.

Exercise 3-1. Modify the program sum3 to ignore blank lines. ☐

Exercise 3-2. Add the more general regular expression for a number. How does it affect the running time? ☐

Exercise 3-3. What is the effect of removing the test of numcol in the second for statement? ☐

Exercise 3-4. Write a program that reads a list of item and quantity pairs and for each item on the list accumulates the total quantity; at the end, it prints the items and total quantities, sorted alphabetically by item. ☐

Computing Percentages and Quantiles

Suppose that we want not the sum of a column of numbers but what percentage each is of the total. This requires two passes over the data. If there's only one column of numbers and not too much data, the easiest way is to store the numbers in an array on the first pass, then compute the percentages on the second pass as the values are being printed:

```
# percent
#    input:   a column of nonnegative numbers
#    output:  each number and its percentage of the total

    { x[NR] = $1; sum += $1 }

END { if (sum != 0)
          for (i = 1; i <= NR; i++)
              printf("%10.2f %5.1f\n", x[i], 100*x[i]/sum)
    }
```

This same approach, though with a more complicated transformation, could be used, for example, in adjusting student grades to fit some curve. Once the grades have been computed (as numbers between 0 and 100), it might be interesting to see a histogram:

```
# histogram
#    input:   numbers between 0 and 100
#    output:  histogram of deciles

    { x[int($1/10)]++ }

END { for (i = 0; i < 10; i++)
          printf(" %2d - %2d: %3d %s\n",
              10*i, 10*i+9, x[i], rep(x[i],"*"))
      printf("100:      %3d %s\n", x[10], rep(x[10],"*"))
    }

function rep(n,s,   t) {   # return string of n s's
    while (n-- > 0)
        t = t s
    return t
}
```

Note how the postfix decrement operator -- is used to control the while loop.

We can test histogram with some randomly generated grades. The first program in the pipeline below generates 200 random numbers between 0 and 100, and pipes them into the histogram maker.

```
awk '
# generate random integers
BEGIN { for (i = 1; i <= 200; i++)
            print int(101*rand())
      }
' |
awk -f histogram
```

It produces this output:

```
  0 -   9:  21 *********************
 10 -  19:  20 ********************
 20 -  29:  15 ***************
 30 -  39:  29 *****************************
 40 -  49:  23 ***********************
 50 -  59:  16 ****************
 60 -  69:  16 ****************
 70 -  79:  20 ********************
 80 -  89:  12 ************
 90 -  99:  27 ***************************
100:        1 *
```

Exercise 3-5. Scale the rows of stars so they don't overflow the line length when there's a lot of data. □

Exercise 3-6. Make a version of the histogram code that divides the input into a specified number of buckets, adjusting the ranges according to the data seen. □

Numbers with Commas

Suppose we have a list of numbers that contain commas and decimal points, like 12,345.67. Since awk thinks that the first comma terminates a number, these numbers cannot be summed directly. The commas must first be erased:

```
# sumcomma - add up numbers containing commas

    { gsub(/,/, ""); sum += $0 }
END { print sum }
```

The effect of gsub(/,/, "") is to replace every comma with the null string, that is, to delete the commas.

This program doesn't check that the commas are in the right places, nor does it print commas in its answer. Putting commas into numbers requires only a little effort, as the next program shows. It formats numbers with commas and two digits after the decimal point. The structure of this program is a useful one to emulate: it contains a function that only does the new thing, with the rest of the program just reading and printing. After it's been tested and is working, the new function can be included in the final program.

The basic idea is to insert commas from the decimal point to the left in a loop; each iteration puts a comma in front of the leftmost three digits that are followed by a comma or decimal point, provided there will be at least one additional digit in front of the comma. The algorithm uses recursion to handle negative numbers: if the input is negative, the function addcomma calls itself with the positive value, tacks on a leading minus sign, and returns the result.

```
# addcomma - put commas in numbers
#    input:  a number per line
#    output: the input number followed by
#           the number with commas and two decimal places

{ printf("%-12s %20s\n", $0, addcomma($0)) }

function addcomma(x,    num) {
    if (x < 0)
        return "-" addcomma(-x)
    num = sprintf("%.2f", x)    # num is dddddd.dd
    while (num ~ /[0-9][0-9][0-9][0-9]/)
        sub(/[0-9][0-9][0-9][,.]/, ",&", num)
    return num
}
```

Note the use of the & in the replacement text for sub to add a comma before each triplet of numbers.

Here are the results for some test data:

```
0                              0.00
-1                            -1.00
-12.34                       -12.34
12345                     12,345.00
-1234567.89           -1,234,567.89
-123.                       -123.00
-123456                 -123,456.00
```

Exercise 3-7. Modify sumcomma, the program that adds numbers with commas, to check that the commas in the numbers are properly positioned. □

Fixed-Field Input

Information appearing in fixed-width fields often requires some kind of preprocessing before it can be used directly. Some programs, such as spreadsheets, put out numbers in fixed columns, rather than with field separators; if the numbers are too wide, the columns abut. Fixed-field data is best handled with substr, which can be used to pick apart any combination of columns. For example, suppose the first six characters of each line contain a date in the form mmddyy. The easiest way to sort this by date is to convert the dates into the form yymmdd:

```
# date convert - convert mmddyy into yymmdd in $1

{ $1 = substr($1,5,2) substr($1,1,2) substr($1,3,2); print }
```

On input sorted by month, like this:

```
013042 mary's birthday
032772 mark's birthday
052470 anniversary
061209 mother's birthday
110175 elizabeth's birthday
```

it produces the output

```
420130 mary's birthday
720327 mark's birthday
700524 anniversary
090612 mother's birthday
751101 elizabeth's birthday
```

which is ready to be sorted by year, month and day.

Exercise 3-8. How would you convert dates into a form in which you can do arithmetic like computing the number of days between two dates? □

Program Cross-Reference Checking

Awk is often used to extract information from the output of other programs. Sometimes that output is merely a set of homogeneous lines, in which case field-splitting or substr operations are quite adequate. Sometimes, however, the upstream program thinks its output is intended for people. In that case, the task of the awk program is to undo careful formatting, so as to extract the information from the irrelevant. The next example is a simple instance.

Large programs are built from many files. It is convenient (and sometimes vital) to know which file defines which function, and where the function is used. To that end, the Unix program nm prints a neatly formatted list of the names, definitions, and uses of the names in a set of object files. A typical fragment of its output looks like this:

```
file.o:
00000c80 T _addroot
00000b30 T _checkdev
00000a3c T _checkdupl
         U _chown
         U _client
         U _close
funmount.o:
00000000 T _funmount
         U cerror
```

Lines with one field (e.g., file.o) are filenames, lines with two fields (e.g., U and _close) are uses of names, and lines with three fields are definitions of names. T indicates that a definition is a text symbol (function) and U indicates that the name is undefined.

Using this raw output to determine what file defines or uses a particular symbol can be a nuisance, since the filename is not attached to each symbol. For a C program the list can be long — it's 850 lines for the nine files of source that make up awk itself. A three-line awk program, however, can add the name to each item, so subsequent programs can retrieve the useful information from one line:

```
# nm.format - add filename to each nm output line

NF == 1 { file = $1 }
NF == 2 { print file, $1, $2 }
NF == 3 { print file, $2, $3 }
```

The output from nm.format on the data shown above is

```
file.o: T _addroot
file.o: T _checkdev
file.o: T _checkdupl
file.o: U _chown
file.o: U _client
file.o: U _close
funmount.o: T _funmount
funmount.o: U cerror
```

Now it is easy for other programs to search this output or process it further.

This technique does not provide line number information nor tell how many times a name is used in a file, but these things can be found by a text editor or another awk program. Nor does it depend on which language the programs are written in, so it is much more flexible than the usual run of cross-referencing tools, and shorter and simpler too.

Formatted Output

As another example we'll use awk to make money, or at least to print checks. The input consists of lines, each containing a check number, an amount, and a payee, separated by tabs. The output goes on check forms, eight lines high. The second and third lines have the check number and date indented 45 spaces, the fourth line contains the payee in a field 45 characters long, followed by three blanks, followed by the amount. The fifth line contains the amount in words, and the other lines are blank. A check looks like this:

```
                                        1026
                                        Jun 17, 1987
Pay to Mary R. Worth------------------------------   $123.45
the sum of one hundred twenty three dollars and 45 cents exactly



                                _____
```

Here is the code:

```
# prchecks - print formatted checks
#    input:  number \t amount \t payee
#    output: eight lines of text for preprinted check forms

BEGIN {
    FS = "\t"
    dashes = sp45 = sprintf("%45s", " ")
    gsub(/ /, "-", dashes)             # to protect the payee
    "date" | getline date              # get today's date
    split(date, d, " ")
    date = d[2] " " d[3] ", " d[6]
    initnum()    # set up tables for number conversion
}
NF != 3 || $2 >= 1000000 {             # illegal data
    printf("\nline %d illegal:\n%s\n\nVOID\nVOID\n\n\n", NR, $0)
    next                               # no check printed
}
{   printf("\n")                       # nothing on line 1
    printf("%s%s\n", sp45, $1)         # number, indented 45 spaces
    printf("%s%s\n", sp45, date)       # date, indented 45 spaces
    amt = sprintf("%.2f", $2)          # formatted amount
    printf("Pay to %45.45s  $%s\n", $3 dashes, amt) # line 4
    printf("the sum of %s\n", numtowords(amt))      # line 5
    printf("\n\n\n")                   # lines 6, 7 and 8
}

function numtowords(n,    cents, dols) { # n has 2 decimal places
    cents = substr(n, length(n)-1, 2)
    dols = substr(n, 1, length(n)-3)
    if (dols == 0)
        return "zero dollars and " cents " cents exactly"
    return intowords(dols) " dollars and " cents " cents exactly"
}

function intowords(n) {
    n = int(n)
    if (n >= 1000)
        return intowords(n/1000) " thousand " intowords(n%1000)
    if (n >= 100)
        return intowords(n/100) " hundred " intowords(n%100)
    if (n >= 20)
        return tens[int(n/10)] " " intowords(n%10)
    return nums[n]
}

function initnum() {
    split("one two three four five six seven eight nine " \
          "ten eleven twelve thirteen fourteen fifteen " \
          "sixteen seventeen eighteen nineteen", nums, " ")
    split("ten twenty thirty forty fifty sixty " \
          "seventy eighty ninety", tens, " ")
}
```

The program contains several interesting constructs. First, notice how we generate a long string of blanks in the BEGIN action with sprintf, and then convert them to dashes by substitution. Note also how we combine line continuation and string concatenation to create the string argument to split in the function initnum; this is a useful idiom.

The date comes from the system by the line

```
"date" | getline date          # get today's date
```

which runs the date command and pipes its output into getline. A little processing converts the date from

```
Wed Jun 17 13:39:36 EDT 1987
```

into

```
Jun 17, 1987
```

(This may need revision on non-Unix systems that do not support pipes.)

The functions numtowords and intowords convert numbers to words. They are straightforward, although about half the program is devoted to them. The function intowords is recursive: it calls itself to deal with a simpler part of the problem. This is the second example of recursion in this chapter, and we will see others later on. In each case, recursion is an effective way to break a big job into smaller, more manageable pieces.

Exercise 3-9. Use the function addcomma from a previous example to include commas in the printed amount. □

Exercise 3-10. The program prchecks does not deal with negative quantities or very long amounts in a graceful way. Modify the program to reject requests for checks for negative amounts and to split very long amounts onto two lines. □

Exercise 3-11. The function numtowords sometimes puts out two blanks in a row. It also produces blunders like "one dollars." How would you fix these defects? □

Exercise 3-12. Modify the program to put hyphens into the proper places in spelled-out amounts, as in "twenty-one dollars." □

3.2 Data Validation

Another common use for awk programs is data validation: making sure that data is legal or at least plausible. This section contains several small programs that check input for validity. For example, consider the column-summing programs in the previous section. Are there any numeric fields where there should be nonnumeric ones, or vice versa? Such a program is very close to one we saw before, with the summing removed:

```
# colcheck - check consistency of columns
#    input:  rows of numbers and strings
#    output: lines whose format differs from first line

NR == 1 {
    nfld = NF
    for (i = 1; i <= NF; i++)
        type[i] = isnum($i)
}
{   if (NF != nfld)
        printf("line %d has %d fields instead of %d\n",
            NR, NF, nfld)
    for (i = 1; i <= NF; i++)
        if (isnum($i) != type[i])
            printf("field %d in line %d differs from line 1\n",
                i, NR)
}

function isnum(n) { return n ~ /^[+-]?[0-9]+$/ }
```

The test for numbers is again just a sequence of digits with an optional sign; see the discussion of regular expressions in Section 2.1 for a more complete version.

Balanced Delimiters

In the machine-readable text of this book, each program is introduced by a line beginning with .P1 and is terminated by a line beginning with .P2. These lines are text-formatting commands that make the programs come out in their distinctive font when the text is typeset. Since programs cannot be nested, these text-formatting commands must form an alternating sequence

```
.P1 .P2 .P1 .P2 ... .P1 .P2
```

If one or the other of these delimiters is omitted, the output will be badly mangled by our text formatter. To make sure that the programs would be typeset properly, we wrote this tiny delimiter checker, which is typical of a large class of such programs:

```
# p12check - check input for alternating .P1/.P2 delimiters

/^\.P1/ { if (p != 0)
              print ".P1 after .P1, line", NR
          p = 1
        }
/^\.P2/ { if (p != 1)
              print ".P2 with no preceding .P1, line", NR
          p = 0
        }
END     { if (p != 0) print "missing .P2 at end" }
```

If the delimiters are in the right order, the variable p silently goes through the sequence of values 0 1 0 1 0 ... 1 0. Otherwise, the appropriate error messages are printed.

Exercise 3-13. What is the best way to extend this program to handle multiple sets of delimiter pairs? □

Password-File Checking

The password file on a Unix system contains the name of and other information about authorized users. Each line of the password file has 7 fields, separated by colons:

```
root:qyxRi2uhuVjrg:0:2::/:
bwk:1L./v6iblzzNE:9:1:Brian Kernighan:/usr/bwk:
ava:otxs1oTVoyvMQ:15:1:Al Aho:/usr/ava:
uucp:xutIBs2hKtcls:48:1:uucp daemon:/usr/lib/uucp:uucico
pjw:xNqy//GDc8FFg:170:2:Peter Weinberger:/usr/pjw:
mark:j0z1fuQmqIvdE:374:1:Mark Kernighan:/usr/bwk/mark:
...
```

The first field is the user's login name, which should be alphanumeric. The second is an encrypted version of the password; if this field is empty, anyone can log in pretending to be that user, while if there is a password, only people who know the password can log in. The third and fourth fields are supposed to be numeric. The sixth field should begin with /. The following program prints all lines that fail to satisfy these criteria, along with the number of the erroneous line and an appropriate diagnostic message. Running this program every night is a small part of keeping a system healthy and safe from intruders.

```
# passwd - check password file

BEGIN {
    FS = ":" }
NF != 7 {
    printf("line %d, does not have 7 fields: %s\n", NR, $0) }
$1 ~ /[^A-Za-z0-9]/ {
    printf("line %d, nonalphanumeric user id: %s\n", NR, $0) }
$2 == "" {
    printf("line %d, no password: %s\n", NR, $0) }
$3 ~ /[^0-9]/ {
    printf("line %d, nonnumeric user id: %s\n", NR, $0) }
$4 ~ /[^0-9]/ {
    printf("line %d, nonnumeric group id: %s\n", NR, $0) }
$6 !~ /^\// {
    printf("line %d, invalid login directory: %s\n", NR, $0) }
```

This is a good example of a program that can be developed incrementally: each time someone thinks of a new condition that should be checked, it can be added, so the program steadily becomes more thorough.

Generating Data-Validation Programs

We constructed the password-file checking program by hand, but a more interesting approach is to convert a set of conditions and messages into a checking program automatically. Here is a small set of error conditions and messages, where each condition is a pattern from the program above. The error message is to be printed for each input line where the condition is true.

```
NF != 7                     does not have 7 fields
$1 ~ /[^A-Za-z0-9]/         nonalphanumeric user id
$2 == ""                    no password
```

The following program converts these condition-message pairs into a checking program:

```
# checkgen - generate data-checking program
#     input:  expressions of the form: pattern tabs message
#     output: program to print message when pattern matches

BEGIN { FS = "\t+" }
{ printf("%s {\n\tprintf(\"line %%d, %s: %%s\\n\",NR,$0) }\n",
    $1, $2)
}
```

The output is a sequence of conditions and the actions to print the corresponding messages:

```
NF != 7 {
        printf("line %d, does not have 7 fields: %s\n",NR,$0) }
$1 ~ /[^A-Za-z0-9]/ {
        printf("line %d, nonalphanumeric user id: %s\n",NR,$0) }
$2 == "" {
        printf("line %d, no password: %s\n",NR,$0) }
```

When the resulting checking program is executed, each condition will be tested on each line, and if it is satisfied, the line number, error message, and input line will be printed. Note that in checkgen, some of the special characters in the printf format string must be quoted to produce a valid generated program. For example, % is preserved by writing %% and \n is created by writing \\n.

This technique in which one awk program creates another is broadly applicable (and of course it's not restricted to awk programs). We will see several more examples of its use throughout this book.

Exercise 3-14. Add a facility to checkgen so that pieces of code can be passed through verbatim, for example, to create a BEGIN action to set the field separator. □

Which Version of AWK?

Awk is often useful for inspecting programs, or for organizing the activities of other testing programs. This section contains a somewhat incestuous example: a program that examines awk programs.

The new version of the language has more built-in variables and functions, so there is a chance that an old program may inadvertently include one of these names, for example, by using as a variable name a word like sub that is now a built-in function. The following program does a reasonable job of detecting such problems in old programs:

```
# compat - check if awk program uses new built-in names

BEGIN { asplit("close system atan2 sin cos rand srand " \
               "match sub gsub", fcns)
        asplit("ARGC ARGV FNR RSTART RLENGTH SUBSEP", vars)
        asplit("do delete function return", keys)
      }

      { line = $0 }

/"/   { gsub(/"([^"]¦\\")*"/, "", line) }       # remove strings,
/\//  { gsub(/\/([^\/]¦\\\/)+\//, "", line) } # reg exprs,
/#/   { sub(/#.*/, "", line) }                  # and comments

      { n = split(line, x, "[^A-Za-z0-9_]+")  # into words
        for (i = 1; i <= n; i++) {
            if (x[i] in fcns)
                warn(x[i] " is now a built-in function")
            if (x[i] in vars)
                warn(x[i] " is now a built-in variable")
            if (x[i] in keys)
                warn(x[i] " is now a keyword")
        }
      }

function asplit(str, arr) {  # make an assoc array from str
    n = split(str, temp)
    for (i = 1; i <= n; i++)
        arr[temp[i]]++
    return n
}

function warn(s) {
    sub(/^[ \t]*/, "")
    printf("file %s, line %d: %s\n\t%s\n", FILENAME, FNR, s, $0)
}
```

The only real complexity in this program is in the substitution commands that attempt to remove quoted strings, regular expressions, and comments before an input line is checked. This job isn't done perfectly, so some lines may not be properly processed.

The third argument of the first split function is a string that is interpreted as a regular expression. The leftmost longest substrings matched by this regular expression in the input line become the field separators. The split command divides the resulting input line into alphanumeric strings by using nonalphanumeric strings as the field separator; this removes all the operators and punctuation at once.

The function `asplit` is just like `split`, except that it creates an array whose *subscripts* are the words within the string. Incoming words can then be tested for membership in this array.

This is the output of `compat` on itself:

```
file compat, line 12: gsub is now a built-in function
    /\//   { gsub(/\/([^\/]|\\\/)+\//, "", line) } # reg exprs,
file compat, line 13: sub is now a built-in function
    /#/    { sub(/#.*/, "", line) }                 # and comments
file compat, line 26: function is now a keyword
    function asplit(str, arr) {  # make an assoc array from str
file compat, line 30: return is now a keyword
    return n
file compat, line 33: function is now a keyword
    function warn(s) {
file compat, line 34: sub is now a built-in function
    sub(/^[ \t]*/, "")
file compat, line 35: FNR is now a built-in variable
    printf("file %s, line %d: %s\n\t%s\n", FILENAME, FNR, s, $0)
```

Exercise 3-15. Rewrite `compat` to identify keywords, etc., with regular expressions instead of the function `asplit`. Compare the two versions on complexity and speed. □

Exercise 3-16. Because awk variables are not declared, a misspelled name will not be detected. Write a program to identify names that are used only once. To make it truly useful, you will have to handle function declarations and variables used in functions. □

3.3 Bundle and Unbundle

Before discussing multiline records, let's consider a special case. The problem is to combine ("bundle") a set of ASCII files into one file in such a way that they can be easily separated ("unbundled") into the original files. This section contains two tiny awk programs that do this pair of operations. They can be used for bundling small files together to save disk space, or to package a collection of files for convenient electronic mailing.

The `bundle` program is trivial, so short that you can just type it on a command line. All it does is prefix each line of the output with the name of the file, which comes from the built-in variable `FILENAME`.

```
# bundle - combine multiple files into one

{ print FILENAME, $0 }
```

The matching `unbundle` is only a little more elaborate:

```
# unbundle - unpack a bundle into separate files

$1 != prev { close(prev); prev = $1 }
            { print substr($0, index($0, " ") + 1) >$1 }
```

The first line of unbundle closes the previous file when a new one is encountered; if bundles don't contain many files (less than the limit on the number of open files), this line isn't necessary.

There are other ways to write bundle and unbundle, but the versions here are the easiest, and for short files, reasonably space efficient. Another organization is to add a distinctive line with the filename before each file, so the filename appears only once.

Exercise 3-17. Compare the speed and space requirements of these versions of bundle and unbundle with variations that use headers and perhaps trailers. Evaluate the tradeoff between performance and program complexity. □

3.4   Multiline Records

The examples so far have featured data where each record fits neatly on one line. Many other kinds of data, however, come in multiline chunks. Examples include address lists:

```
Adam Smith
1234 Wall St., Apt. 5C
New York, NY 10021
212 555-4321
```

or bibliographic citations:

```
Donald E. Knuth
The Art of Computer Programming
Volume 2: Seminumerical Algorithms, Second Edition
Addison-Wesley, Reading, Mass.
1981
```

or personal databases:

```
Chateau Lafite Rothschild 1947
12 bottles @ 12.95
```

It's easy to create and maintain such information if it's of modest size and regular structure; in effect, each record is the equivalent of an index card. Dealing with such data in awk requires only a bit more work than single-line data does; we'll show several approaches.

Records Separated by Blank Lines

Imagine an address list, where each record contains on the first four lines a name, street address, city and state, and phone number; after these, there may be additional lines of other information. Records are separated by a single blank line:

```
Adam Smith
1234 Wall St., Apt. 5C
New York, NY 10021
212 555-4321

David W. Copperfield
221 Dickens Lane
Monterey, CA 93940
408 555-0041
work phone 408 555-6532
Mary, birthday January 30

Canadian Consulate
555 Fifth Ave
New York, NY
212 586-2400
```

When records are separated by blank lines, they can be manipulated directly: if the record separator variable RS is set to null (RS=""), each multi-line group becomes a record. Thus

```
BEGIN { RS = "" }
/New York/
```

will print each record that contains New York, regardless of how many lines it has:

```
Adam Smith
1234 Wall St., Apt. 5C
New York, NY 10021
212 555-4321
Canadian Consulate
555 Fifth Ave
New York, NY
212 586-2400
```

When several records are printed in this way, there is no blank line between them, so the input format is not preserved. The easiest way to fix this is to set the output record separator ORS to a double newline \n\n:

```
BEGIN { RS = ""; ORS = "\n\n" }
/New York/
```

Suppose we want to print the names and phone numbers of all Smith's, that is, the first and fourth lines of all records in which the first line ends with Smith. That would be easy if each line were a field. This can be arranged by setting FS to \n:

```
BEGIN            { RS = ""; FS = "\n" }
$1 ~ /Smith$/ { print $1, $4 }    # name, phone
```

This produces

```
Adam Smith 212 555-4321
```

Recall that newline is always a field separator for multiline records, regardless
of the value of FS. When RS is set to "", the field separator by default is any
sequence of blanks and tabs, or newline. When FS is set to \n, only a newline
acts as a field separator.

Processing Multiline Records

If an existing program can process its input only by lines, we may still be
able to use it for multiline records by writing two awk programs. The first combines the multiline records into single-line records that can be processed by the
existing program. Then, the second transforms the processed output back into
the original multiline format. (We'll assume that limits on line lengths are not
a problem.)

To illustrate, let's sort our address list with the Unix sort command. The
following pipeline sorts the address list by last name:

```
# pipeline to sort address list by last names

awk '
BEGIN { RS = ""; FS = "\n" }
      { printf("%s!!#", x[split($1, x, " ")])
        for (i = 1; i <= NF; i++)
            printf("%s%s", $i, i < NF ? "!!#" : "\n")
      }
' |
sort |
awk '
BEGIN { FS = "!!#" }
      { for (i = 2; i <= NF; i++)
            printf("%s\n", $i)
        printf("\n")
      }
'
```

In the first program, the function split($1, x, " ") splits the first line of
each record into the array x and returns the number of elements created; thus,
x[split($1, x, " ")] is the entry for the last name. (This assumes that
the last word on the first line really is the last name.) For each multiline record
the first program creates a single line consisting of the last name, followed by
the string !!#, followed by all the fields in the record separated by this string.
Any other separator that does not occur in the data and that sorts earlier than
the data could be used in place of the string !!#. The program after the sort
reconstructs the multiline records using this separator to identify the original

fields.

Exercise 3-18. Modify the first awk program to detect occurrences of the magic string ! ! # in the data. □

Records with Headers and Trailers

Sometimes records are identified by a header and trailer, rather than by a record separator. Consider a simple example, again an address list, but this time each record begins with a header that indicates some characteristic, such as occupation, of the person whose name follows, and each record (except possibly the last) is terminated by a trailer consisting of a blank line:

```
accountant
Adam Smith
1234 Wall St., Apt. 5C
New York, NY 10021

doctor - ophthalmologist
Dr. Will Seymour
798 Maple Blvd.
Berkeley Heights, NJ 07922

lawyer
David W. Copperfield
221 Dickens Lane
Monterey, CA 93940

doctor - pediatrician
Dr. Susan Mark
600 Mountain Avenue
Murray Hill, NJ 07974
```

A range pattern is the simplest way to print the records of all doctors:

```
/^doctor/, /^$/
```

The range pattern matches records that begin with `doctor` and end with a blank line (`/^$/` matches a blank line).

To print the doctor records without headers, we can use

```
/^doctor/ { p = 1; next }
p == 1
/^$/       { p = 0; next }
```

This program uses a variable p to control the printing of lines. When a line containing the desired header is found, p is set to one; a subsequent line containing a trailer resets p to zero, its default initial value. Since lines are printed only when p is set to one, only the body and trailer of each record are printed; other combinations are easily selected instead.

Name-Value Data

In some applications data may have more structure than can be captured by a sequence of unformatted lines. For instance, addresses might include a country name, or might not have a street address.

One way to deal with structured data is to add an identifying name or keyword to each field of each record. For example, here is how we might organize a checkbook in this format:

```
check     1021
to        Champagne Unlimited
amount    123.10
date      1/1/87

deposit
amount    500.00
date      1/1/87

check     1022
date      1/2/87
amount    45.10
to        Getwell Drug Store
tax       medical

check     1023
amount    125.00
to        International Travel
date      1/3/87

amount    50.00
to        Carnegie Hall
date      1/3/87
check     1024
tax       charitable contribution

to        American Express
check     1025
amount    75.75
date      1/5/87
```

We are still using multiline records separated by a single blank line, but within each record, every piece of data is self-identifying: each field consists of an item name, a tab, and the information. That means that different records can contain different fields, or similar fields in arbitrary order.

One way to process this kind of data is to treat it as single lines, with occasional blank lines as separators. Each line identifies the value it corresponds to, but they are not otherwise connected. So to accumulate the sums of deposits and checks, for example, we could simply scan the input for deposits and checks, like this:

```
# check1 - print total deposits and checks

/^check/    { ck = 1; next }
/^deposit/  { dep = 1; next }
/^amount/   { amt = $2; next }
/^$/        { addup() }

END         { addup()
              printf("deposits $%.2f, checks $%.2f\n",
                  deposits, checks)
            }

function addup() {
    if (ck)
        checks += amt
    else if (dep)
        deposits += amt
    ck = dep = amt = 0
}
```

which produces

```
deposits $500.00, checks $418.95
```

This is easy, and it works (on correct input) no matter what order the items of a record appear in. But it is delicate, requiring careful initialization, reinitialization, and end-of-file processing. Thus an appealing alternative is to read each record as a unit, then pick it apart as needed. The following program computes the same sums of deposits and checks, using a function to extract the value associated with an item of a given name:

```
# check2 - print total deposits and checks

BEGIN               { RS = ""; FS = "\n" }
/(^|\n)deposit/     { deposits += field("amount"); next }
/(^|\n)check/       { checks += field("amount"); next }
END                 { printf("deposits $%.2f, checks $%.2f\n",
                          deposits, checks)
                    }

function field(name,    i,f) {
    for (i = 1; i <= NF; i++) {
        split($i, f, "\t")
        if (f[1] == name)
            return f[2]
    }
    printf("error: no field %s in record\n%s\n", name, $0)
}
```

The function field(s) finds an item in the current record whose name is s; it returns the value associated with that name.

A third possibility is to split each field into an associative array and access that for the values. To illustrate, here is a program that prints the check information in a more compact form:

```
1/1/87   1021   $123.10   Champagne Unlimited
1/2/87   1022   $45.10    Getwell Drug Store
1/3/87   1023   $125.00   International Travel
1/3/87   1024   $50.00    Carnegie Hall
1/5/87   1025   $75.75    American Express
```

The program is:

```
# check3 - print check information

BEGIN { RS = ""; FS = "\n" }
/(^|\n)check/ {
    for (i = 1; i <= NF; i++) {
        split($i, f, "\t")
        val[f[1]] = f[2]
    }
    printf("%8s %5d %8s  %s\n",
        val["date"],
        val["check"],
        sprintf("$%.2f", val["amount"]),
        val["to"])
    for (i in val)
        delete val[i]
}
```

Note the use of `sprintf` to put a dollar sign in front of the amount; the result-ing string is then right-justified by `printf`.

Exercise 3-19. Write a command `lookup` *x* *y* that will print from a known file all multiline records having the item name *x* with value *y*. □

3.5 Summary

In this chapter, we've presented programs for a variety of different data-processing applications: fetching information from address lists, computing sim-ple statistics from numerical data, checking data and programs for validity, and so forth. There are several reasons why such diverse tasks are fairly easy to do in awk. The pattern-action model is a good match to this kind of processing. The adjustable field and record separators accommodate data in a variety of shapes and formats; associative arrays are convenient for storing both numbers and strings; functions like `split` and `substr` are good at picking apart textual data; and `printf` is a flexible output formatter. In the following chapters, we'll see further applications of these facilities.

4   REPORTS AND DATABASES

This chapter shows how awk can be used to extract information and generate reports from data stored in files. The emphasis is on tabular data, but the techniques apply to more complex forms as well. The theme is the development of programs that can be used with one another. We will see a number of common data-processing problems that are hard to solve in one step, but easily handled by making several passes over the data.

The first part of the chapter deals with generating reports by scanning a single file. Although the format of the final report is of primary interest, there are complexities in the scanning too. The second part of the chapter describes one approach to collecting data from several interrelated files. We've chosen to do this in a fairly general way, by thinking of the group of files as a relational database. One of the advantages is that fields can have names instead of numbers.

4.1 Generating Reports

Awk can be used to select data from files and then to format the selected data into a report. We will use a three-step process to generate reports: prepare, sort, format. The preparation step involves selecting data and perhaps performing computations on it to obtain the desired information. The sort step is necessary if we want to order the data in some particular fashion. To perform this step we pass the output of the preparation program into the system sort command. The formatting step is done by a second awk program that generates the desired report from the sorted data. In this section we will generate a few reports from the countries file of Chapter 2 to illustrate the approach.

A Simple Report

Suppose we want a report giving the population, area, and population density of each country. We would like the countries to be grouped by continent, and the continents to be sorted alphabetically; within each continent the countries are to be listed in decreasing order of population density, like this:

CONTINENT	COUNTRY	POPULATION	AREA	POP. DEN.
Asia	Japan	120	144	833.3
Asia	India	746	1267	588.8
Asia	China	1032	3705	278.5
Asia	USSR	275	8649	31.8
Europe	Germany	61	96	635.4
Europe	England	56	94	595.7
Europe	France	55	211	260.7
North America	Mexico	78	762	102.4
North America	USA	237	3615	65.6
North America	Canada	25	3852	6.5
South America	Brazil	134	3286	40.8

The first two steps in preparing this report are done by the program prep1, which, when applied to the file countries, determines the relevant information and sorts it:

```
# prep1 - prepare countries by continent and pop. den.

BEGIN { FS = "\t" }
      { printf("%s:%s:%d:%d:%.1f\n",
            $4, $1, $3, $2, 1000*$3/$2) | "sort -t: +0 -1 +4rn"
      }
```

The output is a sequence of lines containing five fields, separated by colons, that give the continent, country, population, area, and population density:

```
Asia:Japan:120:144:833.3
Asia:India:746:1267:588.8
Asia:China:1032:3705:278.5
Asia:USSR:275:8649:31.8
Europe:Germany:61:96:635.4
Europe:England:56:94:595.7
Europe:France:55:211:260.7
North America:Mexico:78:762:102.4
North America:USA:237:3615:65.6
North America:Canada:25:3852:6.5
South America:Brazil:134:3286:40.8
```

We wrote prep1 to print directly into the Unix sort command. The -t: argument tells sort to use a colon as its field separator. The +0 -1 arguments make the first field the primary sort key. The +4rn argument makes the fifth field, in reverse numeric order, the secondary sort key. (In Section 6.3, we will show a sort-generator program that creates these lists of options from a description in words.)

If your system does not support printing into a pipe, remove the sort command and just print into a file with print >*file*; the file can be sorted in a separate step. This applies to all the examples in this chapter.

We have completed the preparation and sort steps; all we need now is to format this information into the desired report. The program form1 does the job:

```
# form1 - format countries data by continent, pop. den.

BEGIN { FS = ":"
        printf("%-15s %-10s %10s %7s %12s\n",
            "CONTINENT", "COUNTRY", "POPULATION",
            "AREA", "POP. DEN.")
      }
      { printf("%-15s %-10s %7d %10d %10.1f\n",
            $1, $2, $3, $4, $5)
      }
```

The desired report can be generated by typing the command line

```
awk -f prep1 countries ¦ awk -f form1
```

The peculiar arguments to `sort` in `prep1` can be avoided by having the program format its output so that `sort` doesn't need any arguments, and then having the formatting program reformat the lines. By default, the `sort` command sorts its input lexicographically. In the final report, the output needs to be sorted alphabetically by continent and in reverse numerical order by population density. To avoid arguments to `sort`, the preparation program can put at the beginning of each line a quantity depending on continent and population density that, when sorted lexicographically, will automatically order the output correctly. One possibility is a fixed-width representation of the continent followed by the reciprocal of the population density, as in `prep2`:

```
# prep2 - prepare countries by continent, inverse pop. den.

BEGIN { FS = "\t" }
      { den = 1000*$3/$2
        printf("%-15s:%12.8f:%s:%d:%d:%.1f\n",
            $4, 1/den, $1, $3, $2, den) ¦ "sort"
      }
```

With the `countries` file as input, here is the output from `prep2`:

```
Asia            :   0.00120000:Japan:120:144:833.3
Asia            :   0.00169839:India:746:1267:588.8
Asia            :   0.00359012:China:1032:3705:278.5
Asia            :   0.03145091:USSR:275:8649:31.8
Europe          :   0.00157377:Germany:61:96:635.4
Europe          :   0.00167857:England:56:94:595.7
Europe          :   0.00383636:France:55:211:260.7
North America   :   0.00976923:Mexico:78:762:102.4
North America   :   0.01525316:USA:237:3615:65.6
North America   :   0.15408000:Canada:25:3852:6.5
South America   :   0.02452239:Brazil:134:3286:40.8
```

The format `%-15s` is wide enough for all the continent names, and `%12.8f` covers a wide range of reciprocal densities. The final formatting program is like `form1` but skips the new second field. The trick of manufacturing a sort key that simplifies the sorting options is quite general. We'll use it again in an indexing program in Chapter 5.

If we would like a slightly fancier report in which only the first occurrence of each continent name is printed, we can use the formatting program form2 in place of form1:

```
# form2 - format countries by continent, pop. den.

BEGIN { FS = ":"
        printf("%-15s %-10s %10s %7s %12s\n",
            "CONTINENT", "COUNTRY", "POPULATION",
            "AREA", "POP. DEN.")
      }
{ if ($1 != prev) {
        print ""
        prev = $1
    } else
        $1 = ""
    printf("%-15s %-10s %7d %10d %10.1f\n",
        $1, $2, $3, $4, $5)
}
```

The command line

```
awk -f prep1 countries | awk -f form2
```

generates this report:

CONTINENT	COUNTRY	POPULATION	AREA	POP. DEN.
Asia	Japan	120	144	833.3
	India	746	1267	588.8
	China	1032	3705	278.5
	USSR	275	8649	31.8
Europe	Germany	61	96	635.4
	England	56	94	595.7
	France	55	211	260.7
North America	Mexico	78	762	102.4
	USA	237	3615	65.6
	Canada	25	3852	6.5
South America	Brazil	134	3286	40.8

The formatting program form2 is a "control-break" program. The variable prev keeps track of the value of the continent field; only when it changes is the continent name printed. In the next section, we will see a more complicated example of control-break programming.

A More Complex Report

Typical business reports have more substance (or at least form) than what we have seen so far. To illustrate, suppose we want continent subtotals and information about the percentage contributed by each country to the total population and area. We would also like to add a title and more column headers:

Report No. 3	POPULATION, AREA, POPULATION DENSITY				January 1, 1988
CONTINENT	COUNTRY	POPULATION		AREA	POP. DEN.
		Millions of People	Pct. of Total	Thousands of Sq. Mi.	Pct. of Total	People per Sq. Mi.
		---------	-------	----------	-------	----------
Asia	Japan	120	4.3	144	0.6	833.3
	India	746	26.5	1267	4.9	588.8
	China	1032	36.6	3705	14.4	278.5
	USSR	275	9.8	8649	33.7	31.8
		----	-----	-----	-----	
TOTAL for Asia		2173	77.1	13765	53.6	
		====	=====	=====	=====	
Europe	Germany	61	2.2	96	0.4	635.4
	England	56	2.0	94	0.4	595.7
	France	55	2.0	211	0.8	260.7
		----	-----	-----	-----	
TOTAL for Europe		172	6.1	401	1.6	
		====	=====	=====	=====	
North America	Mexico	78	2.8	762	3.0	102.4
	USA	237	8.4	3615	14.1	65.6
	Canada	25	0.9	3852	15.0	6.5
		----	-----	-----	-----	
TOTAL for North America		340	12.1	8229	32.0	
		====	=====	=====	=====	
South America	Brazil	134	4.8	3286	12.8	40.8
		----	-----	-----	-----	
TOTAL for South America		134	4.8	3286	12.8	
		====	=====	=====	=====	
GRAND TOTAL		2819	100.0	25681	100.0	
		=====	======	=====	======	

We can also generate this report using the prepare-sort-format strategy; prep3 prepares and sorts the necessary information from the countries file:

```
# prep3 - prepare countries data for form3

BEGIN  { FS = "\t" }
pass == 1 {
    area[$4] += $2
    areatot += $2
    pop[$4] += $3
    poptot += $3
}
pass == 2 {
    den = 1000*$3/$2
    printf("%s:%s:%s:%f:%d:%f:%f:%d:%d\n",
        $4, $1, $3, 100*$3/poptot, $2, 100*$2/areatot,
        den, pop[$4], area[$4]) ¦ "sort -t: +0 -1 +6rn"
}
```

This program needs two passes over the data. In the first pass it accumulates the area and population of each continent in the arrays area and pop, and also the totals areatot and poptot. In the second pass it formats the result for each country and pipes it into `sort`. The two passes are controlled by the value of the variable `pass`, which can be changed on the command line between passes:

```
awk -f prep3 pass=1 countries pass=2 countries
```

The output of `prep3` consists of lines with 9 colon-separated fields:

    continent
    country
    population
    percentage of total population
    area
    percentage of total area
    population density
    total population of this country's continent
    total area of this country's continent

Note that we've reverted to using tricky arguments to the sort command: the records are piped into `sort`, which sorts them alphabetically by the first field and in reverse numeric order by the seventh field.

The fancy report can be generated by typing the command line

```
awk -f prep3 pass=1 countries pass=2 countries ¦ awk -f form3
```

where the program `form3` is:

```
# form3 - format countries report number 3

BEGIN   {
    FS = ":"; date = "January 1, 1988"
    hfmt = "%36s %8s %12s %7s %12s\n"
    tfmt = "%33s %10s %10s %9s\n"
    TOTfmt = "    TOTAL for %-13s%7d%11.1f%11d%10.1f\n"
    printf("%-18s %-40s %19s\n\n", "Report No. 3",
        "POPULATION, AREA, POPULATION DENSITY", date)
    printf(" %-14s %-14s %-23s %-14s %-11s\n\n",
        "CONTINENT", "COUNTRY", "POPULATION", "AREA", "POP. DEN.")
    printf(hfmt, "Millions ", "Pct. of", "Thousands ",
                "Pct. of", "People per")
    printf(hfmt, "of People", "Total ", "of Sq. Mi.",
                "Total ", "Sq. Mi. ")
    printf(hfmt, "---------", "-------", "----------",
                "-------", "----------")
}
{   if ($1 != prev) { # new continent
        if (NR > 1)
            totalprint()
        prev = $1       # first entry for continent
        poptot = $8;  poppct = $4
        areatot = $9; areapct = $6
    } else {            # next entry for continent
        $1 = ""
```

```
            poppct += $4; areapct += $6
    }
    printf(" %-15s%-10s %6d %10.1f %10d %9.1f %10.1f\n",
        $1, $2, $3, $4, $5, $6, $7)
    gpop += $3;  gpoppct += $4
    garea += $5; gareapct += $6
}

END {
    totalprint()
    printf(" GRAND TOTAL %20d %10.1f %10d %9.1f\n",
        gpop, gpoppct, garea, gareapct)
    printf(tfmt, "=====", "======", "=====", "======")
}

function totalprint() {  # print totals for previous continent
    printf(tfmt, "----", "-----", "-----", "-----")
    printf(TOTfmt, prev, poptot, poppct, areatot, areapct)
    printf(tfmt, "====", "=====", "=====", "=====")
}
```

In addition to formatting, form3 accumulates and prints subtotals for each continent, and also accumulates the total population, population percentage, area, and area percentage, which are printed as part of the action associated with the END pattern.

The form3 program prints a total after all of the entries for each continent have been seen. But naturally it doesn't know that all the entries have been seen until a new continent is encountered. Dealing with this "we've gone too far" situation is the classic example of control-break programming. The solution here is to test each input line before printing, to see whether a total has to be produced for the previous group; the same test has to be included in the END action as well, which means it's best to use a function for the computation. Control breaks are easy enough when there is only one level, but get messier when there are multiple levels.

As these examples suggest, complex formatting tasks can often be done by the composition of awk programs. But it remains an appallingly tedious business to count characters and write printf statements to make everything come out properly lined up, and it's a nightmare when something has to be changed.

An alternative is to let a program compute how big things are, then do the positioning for you. It would be quite feasible to write an awk program to format simple tables for printers; we'll come back to that in a moment. Since we are using Unix and a typesetter, however, we can use what already exists: the tbl program, which does table formatting. The program form4 is very similar to form3, except that it contains no magic numbers for column widths. Instead, it generates some tbl commands and the table data in columns separated by tabs; tbl does the rest. (If you are not familiar with tbl, you can safely ignore the details.)

```
# form4 - format countries data for tbl input

BEGIN   {
    FS = ":"; OFS = "\t"; date = "January 1, 1988"
    print ".TS\ncenter;"
    print "l c s s s r s\nl\nl l c s c s c\nl l c c c c c."
    printf("%s\t%s\t%s\n\n", "Report No. 3",
        "POPULATION, AREA, POPULATION DENSITY", date)
    print "CONTINENT", "COUNTRY", "POPULATION",
        "AREA", "POP. DEN."
    print "", "", "Millions", "Pct. of", "Thousands",
        "Pct. of", "People per"
    print "", "", "of People", "Total", "of Sq. Mi.",
        "Total", "Sq. Mi."
    print "\t\t_\t_ \t_ \t_ \t_ "
    print ".T&\nl l̄ n n̄ n̄ n̄ n."
}

{   if ($1 != prev) {  # new continent
        if (NR > 1)
            totalprint()
        prev = $1
        poptot = $8;  poppct = $4
        areatot = $9; areapct = $6
    } else {              # next entry for current continent
        $1 = ""
        poppct += $4; areapct += $6
    }
    printf("%s\t%s\t%d\t%.1f\t%d\t%.1f\t%.1f\n",
        $1, $2, $3, $4, $5, $6, $7)
    gpop += $3;  gpoppct += $4
    garea += $5; gareapct += $6
}

END {
    totalprint()
    print ".T&\nl s n n n n n."
    printf("GRAND TOTAL\t%d\t%.1f\t%d\t%.1f\n",
        gpop, gpoppct, garea, gareapct)
    print "", "=", "=", "=", "=", "="
    print ".TE"
}

function totalprint() {    # print totals for previous continent
    print ".T&\nl s n n n n n."
    print "", "_", "_", " ", " ", " "
    printf("   TOTAL for %s\t%d\t%.1f\t%d\t%.1f\n",
        prev, poptot, poppct, areatot, areapct)
    print "", "=", "=", "=", "=", "="
    print ".T&\nl l n n n n n."
}
```

When the output from `form4` is run through `tbl`, this table results:

Report No. 3   POPULATION, AREA, POPULATION DENSITY   January 1, 1988

CONTINENT	COUNTRY	POPULATION		AREA		POP. DEN.
		Millions of People	Pct. of Total	Thousands of Sq. Mi.	Pct. of Total	People per Sq. Mi.
Asia	Japan	120	4.3	144	0.6	833.3
	India	746	26.5	1267	4.9	588.8
	China	1032	36.6	3705	14.4	278.5
	USSR	275	9.8	8649	33.7	31.8
TOTAL for Asia		2173	77.1	13765	53.6	
Europe	Germany	61	2.2	96	0.4	635.4
	England	56	2.0	94	0.4	595.7
	France	55	2.0	211	0.8	260.7
TOTAL for Europe		172	6.1	401	1.6	
North America	Mexico	78	2.8	762	3.0	102.4
	USA	237	8.4	3615	14.1	65.6
	Canada	25	0.9	3852	15.0	6.5
TOTAL for North America		340	12.1	8229	32.0	
South America	Brazil	134	4.8	3286	12.8	40.8
TOTAL for South America		134	4.8	3286	12.8	
GRAND TOTAL		2819	100.0	25681	100.0	

We suggested above the possibility of building a program to format tables. Implementing a program as sophisticated as `tbl` is too ambitious, but let's make something smaller: a program that prints items in columns with text items left-justified on the widest entry in that column, and numeric items right justified and centered on the widest entry. In other words, given a header and the `countries` file as input it would print:

```
COUNTRY    AREA    POPULATION    CONTINENT
USSR       8649       275        Asia
Canada     3852        25        North America
China      3705      1032        Asia
USA        3615       237        North America
Brazil     3286       134        South America
India      1267       746        Asia
Mexico      762        78        North America
France      211         55       Europe
Japan       144        120       Asia
Germany      96         61       Europe
England      94         56       Europe
```

The program is fairly compact:

```
# table - simple table formatter
BEGIN {
    FS = "\t"; blanks = sprintf("%100s", " ")
    number = "^[+-]?([0-9]+[.]?[0-9]*|[.][0-9]+)$"
}

{   row[NR] = $0
    for (i = 1; i <= NF; i++) {
        if ($i ~ number)
            nwid[i] = max(nwid[i], length($i))
        wid[i] = max(wid[i], length($i))
    }
}

END {
    for (r = 1; r <= NR; r++) {
        n = split(row[r], d)
        for (i = 1; i <= n; i++) {
            sep = (i < n) ? "    " : "\n"
            if (d[i] ~ number)
                printf("%" wid[i] "s%s", numjust(i,d[i]), sep)
            else
                printf("%-" wid[i] "s%s", d[i], sep)
        }
    }
}

function max(x, y) { return (x > y) ? x : y }

function numjust(n, s) {    # position s in field n
    return s substr(blanks, 1, int((wid[n]-nwid[n])/2))
}
```

The first pass records the data and computes the maximum widths of the numeric and nonnumeric items for each column. The second pass (in the END action) prints each item in the proper position. Left-justifying alphabetic items is easy: we just use wid[i], the maximum width of column i, to build a format string for printf; if the maximum width is 10, for instance, the format will be %-10s for each alphabetic item in column i.

It's a bit more work for numeric items: a numeric item v in column i has to be right-justified like this:

The number of blanks to the right of v is (wid[i]-nwid[i])/2, so numjust concatenates that many blanks to the end of v, then prints it with %10s (again assuming a width of 10).

Exercise 4-1. Modify `form3` and `form4` to use a date provided from elsewhere, rather than having it built in. □

Exercise 4-2. Because of rounding, column entries printed by `form3` and `form4` do not always add up to the subtotals shown. How would you correct this? □

Exercise 4-3. The table formatter assumes that all numbers have the same number of digits after the decimal point. Modify it to work properly if this assumption is not true. □

Exercise 4-4. Enhance `table` to permit a sequence of specification lines that tell how the subsequent data is to be formatted in each column. (This is how `tbl` is controlled.) □

4.2   Packaged Queries and Reports

When a query is asked repeatedly, it makes sense to package it into a command that can be invoked without much typing. Suppose we want to determine the population, area, and population density of various countries. To determine this information for Canada, for example, we could type the command (assuming a Unix-like shell)

```
awk '
BEGIN { FS = "\t" }
$1 ~ /Canada/ {
    printf("%s:\n", $1)
    printf("\t%d million people\n", $3)
    printf("\t%.3f million sq. mi.\n", $2/1000)
    printf("\t%.1f people per sq. mi.\n", 1000*$3/$2)
}
' countries
```

and get the response

```
Canada:
        25 million people
        3.852 million sq. mi.
        6.5 people per sq. mi.
```

Now, if we want to invoke this same command on different countries, we would get tired of substituting the new country name into the awk program every time we executed the command. We would find it more convenient to put the program into an executable file, say `info`, and answer queries by typing

```
info Canada
info USA
...
```

We can use the technique from Section 2.6 to pass the name of the country into the program, or we can use the shell itself to include the country name at the right point:

```
awk '
# info - print information about country
#    usage: info country-name

BEGIN { FS = "\t" }
$1 ~ /'$1'/ {
    printf("%s:\n", $1)
    printf("\t%d million people\n", $3)
    printf("\t%.3f million sq. mi.\n", $2/1000)
    printf("\t%.1f people per sq. mi.\n", 1000*$3/$2)
}
' countries
```

In the beginning of the second line,

```
$1 ~ /'$1'/
```

the first $1 refers to the first field in the input file and the second (apparently quoted) $1 to the country parameter, which is the first argument of the shell command info. The second $1 is visible only to the shell, which replaces it by the string following info when this command is invoked. What's happening is that the shell makes up the awk program by concatenating three strings: two multiline strings bounded by single quotes, and $1, the argument to info.

Notice that any regular expression can be passed to info; in particular, it is possible to retrieve information by specifying only a part of a country name or by specifying several countries at once, as in

```
info 'Can¦USA'
```

Exercise 4-5. Revise the info program so the regular expression is passed in through ARGV instead of by shell manipulations. □

Form Letters

Awk can be used to generate form letters by substituting values for parameters in the text of a form letter:

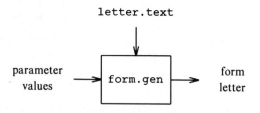

The text of the form letter is stored in the file letter.text. The text contains parameters that will be replaced by a set of parameter values for each form letter that is generated. For example, the following text uses parameters

#1 through #4, which represent the name of a country, and its population, area, and population density:

```
Subject: Demographic Information About #1
From: AWK Demographics, Inc.

In response to your request for information about #1,
our latest research has revealed that its population is #2
million people and its area is #3 million square miles.
This gives #1 a population density of #4 people per
square mile.
```

From the input values

```
Canada:25:3.852:6.5
```

this form letter is generated:

```
Subject: Demographic Information About Canada
From: AWK Demographics, Inc.

In response to your request for information about Canada,
our latest research has revealed that its population is 25
million people and its area is 3.852 million square miles.
This gives Canada a population density of 6.5 people per
square mile.
```

The program form.gen is the form-letter generator:

```
# form.gen - generate form letters
#    input:  prototype file letter.text; data lines
#    output: one form letter per data line

BEGIN {
    FS = ":"
    while (getline <"letter.text" > 0) # read form letter
        form[++n] = $0
}

{    for (i = 1; i <= n; i++) { # read data lines
        temp = form[i]         # each line generates a letter
        for (j = 1; j <= NF; j++)
            gsub("#" j, $j, temp)
        print temp
    }
}
```

The BEGIN action of form.gen reads the text of the form letter from the file letter.text and stores it in the array form; the remaining action reads the input values and uses gsub to substitute these input values in place of the parameters #n in a copy of the stored form letter. Notice how string concatenation is used to create the first argument of gsub.

4.3   A Relational Database System

In this section, we will describe a simple relational database system centered around an awk-like query language called q, a data dictionary called the `relfile`, and a query processor called `qawk` that translates q queries into awk programs.

This system extends awk as a database language in three ways:

Fields are referred to by name rather than by number.

The database can be spread over several files rather than just one.

A sequence of queries can be made interactively.

The advantage of symbolic rather than numeric references to fields is clear — `$area` is more natural than `$2` — but the advantage of storing a database in several files may not be as obvious. A multifile database is easier to maintain, primarily because it is easier to edit a file with a small number of fields than one that contains all of them. Also, with the database system of this section it is possible to restructure the database without having to change the programs that access it. Finally, for simple queries it is more efficient to access a small file than a large one. On the other hand, we have to be careful to change all relevant files whenever we add information to the database, so that it remains consistent.

Up to this point, our database has consisted of a single file named `countries` in which each line has four fields, named `country`, `area`, `population`, and `continent`. Suppose we add to this database a second file called `capitals` where each entry contains the name of a country and its capital city:

```
USSR     Moscow
Canada   Ottawa
China    Beijing
USA      Washington
Brazil   Brasilia
India    New Delhi
Mexico   Mexico City
France   Paris
Japan    Tokyo
Germany  Bonn
England  London
```

As in the `countries` file, a tab has been used to separate the fields.

From these two files, if we want to print the names of the countries in Asia along with their populations and capitals, we would have to scan both files and then piece together the results. For example, this command would work if there is not too much input data:

```
awk ' BEGIN { FS = "\t" }
      FILENAME == "capitals" {
          cap[$1] = $2
      }
      FILENAME == "countries" && $4 == "Asia" {
          print $1, $3, cap[$1]
      }
  ' capitals countries
```

It would certainly be easier if we could just say something like

```
$continent ~ /Asia/ { print $country, $population, $capital }
```

and have a program figure out where the fields are and how to put them together. This is how we would phrase this query in *q*, the language that we will describe shortly.

Natural Joins

It's time for a bit of terminology. In relational databases, a file is called a *table* or *relation* and the columns are called *attributes*. So we might say that the `capitals` table has the attributes `country` and `capital`.

A *natural join*, or join for short, is an operator that combines two tables into one on the basis of their common attributes. The attributes of the resulting table are all the attributes of the two tables being joined, with duplicates removed. If we join the two tables `countries` and `capitals`, we get a single table, let's call it `cc`, that has the attributes

```
    country, area, population, continent, capital
```

For each country that appears in both tables, we get a row in the `cc` table that has the name of the country, followed by its area, population, continent, and then its capital:

```
    Brazil  3286    134     South America   Brasilia
    Canada  3852    25      North America   Ottawa
    China   3705    1032    Asia            Beijing
    England 94      56      Europe          London
    France  211     55      Europe          Paris
    Germany 96      61      Europe          Bonn
    India   1267    746     Asia            New Delhi
    Japan   144     120     Asia            Tokyo
    Mexico  762     78      North America   Mexico City
    USA     3615    237     North America   Washington
    USSR    8649    275     Asia            Moscow
```

The way we implement the join operator is to sort the operand tables on their common attributes and then merge the rows if their values agree on the common attributes, as in the table above. To answer a query involving attributes from several tables, we will first join the tables and then apply the query to the resulting table. That is, when necessary, we create a temporary file.

Thus to answer the query

```
$continent ~ /Asia/ { print $country, $population, $capital }
```

we join the `countries` and `capitals` tables and apply the query to the result. The trick is how, in general, to decide which tables to join.

The actual joining operation can be done by the Unix command `join`, but if you don't have that available, here is a basic version in awk. It joins two files on the attribute in the first field of each. Notice that the join of the two tables

ATT1	ATT2	ATT3
A	w	p
B	x	q
B	y	r
C	z	s

ATT1	ATT4
A	1
A	2
B	3

is the table

ATT1	ATT2	ATT3	ATT4
A	w	p	1
A	w	p	2
B	x	q	3
B	y	r	3

In other words, `join` does not assume that the input tables are equally long, just that they are sorted. It makes an output line for each possible pairing of matching input fields.

```
# join - join file1 file2 on first field
#    input:  two sorted files, tab-separated fields
#    output: natural join of lines with common first field

BEGIN {
    OFS = sep = "\t"
    file2 = ARGV[2]
    ARGV[2] = ""   # read file1 implicitly, file2 explicitly
    eofstat = 1    # end of file status for file2
    if ((ng = getgroup()) <= 0)
        exit       # file2 is empty
}

{   while (prefix($0) > prefix(gp[1]))
        if ((ng = getgroup()) <= 0)
            exit # file2 exhausted
    if (prefix($0) == prefix(gp[1]))   # 1st attributes in file1
        for (i = 1; i <= ng; i++)      #      and file2 match
            print $0, suffix(gp[i])    # print joined line
}
```

```
function getgroup() { # put equal prefix group into gp[1..ng]
    if (getone(file2, gp, 1) <= 0)     # end of file
        return 0
    for (ng = 2; getone(file2, gp, ng) > 0; ng++)
        if (prefix(gp[ng]) != prefix(gp[1])) {
            unget(gp[ng])     # went too far
            return ng-1
        }
    return ng-1
}

function getone(f, gp, n) {   # get next line in gp[n]
    if (eofstat <= 0) # eof or error has occurred
        return 0
    if (ungot) {        # return lookahead line if it exists
        gp[n] = ungotline
        ungot = 0
        return 1
    }
    return eofstat = (getline gp[n] <f)
}

function unget(s)   { ungotline = s; ungot = 1 }
function prefix(s) { return substr(s, 1, index(s, sep) - 1) }
function suffix(s) { return substr(s, index(s, sep) + 1) }
```

The program is called with two arguments, the two input files. Groups of lines with a common first attribute value are read from the second file. If the prefix of the line read from the first file matches the common attribute value of some group, each line of the group gives rise to a joined output line.

The function getgroup puts the next group of lines with a common prefix into the array gp; it calls getone to get each line, and unget to put a line back if it is not part of the group. We have localized the extraction of the first attribute value into the function prefix so it's easy to change.

You should examine the way in which the functions getone and unget implement a pushback or "un-read" of an input line. Before reading a new line, getone checks to see if there is a line that has already been read and stored by unget, and if there is, returns that instead of reading a new one. Pushback is a different way of dealing with a problem that we encountered earlier, reading one too many inputs. In the control-break programs early in this chapter, we delayed processing; here we pretend, through a pair of functions, that we never even saw the extra input.

Exercise 4-6. This version of join does not check for errors or whether the files are sorted. Remedy these defects. How much bigger is the program? □

Exercise 4-7. Implement a version of join that reads one file entirely into memory, then does the join. Which is simpler? □

Exercise 4-8. Modify join so it can join on any field or fields of the input files, and output any selected subset of fields in any order. □

The relfile

In order to ask questions about a database scattered over several tables, we need to know what is contained in each table. We store this information in a file called the `relfile` ("rel" is for relation). The `relfile` contains the names of the tables in the database, the attributes they contain, and the rules for constructing a table if it does not exist. The `relfile` is a sequence of table descriptors of the form:

> *tablename* :
> *attribute*
> *attribute*
>
> ...
> ! *command*
>
> ...

The tablenames and attributes are strings of letters. After the tablename comes a list of the names of the attributes for that table, each prefixed by blanks or tabs. Following the attributes is an optional sequence of commands prefixed by exclamation points that tell how this table is to be constructed. If a table has no commands, a file with that name containing the data of that table is assumed to exist already. Such a table is called a *base* table. Data is entered and updated in the base tables. A table with a sequence of commands appearing after its name in the `relfile` is a *derived* table. Derived tables are constructed when they are needed.

We will use the following `relfile` for our expanded countries database:

```
countries:
        country
        area
        population
        continent
capitals:
        country
        capital
cc:
        country
        area
        population
        continent
        capital
        !sort countries >temp.countries
        !sort capitals >temp.capitals
        !join temp.countries temp.capitals >cc
```

This file says that there are two base tables, `countries` and `capitals`, and one derived table `cc` that is constructed by sorting the base tables into temporary files, then joining them. That is, `cc` is constructed by executing

```
sort countries >temp.countries
sort capitals >temp.capitals
join temp.countries temp.capitals >cc
```

A `relfile` often includes a *universal relation*, a table that contains all the attributes, as the last table in the `relfile`. This ensures that there is one table that contains any combination of attributes. The table `cc` is a universal relation for the countries-capitals database.

A good design for a complex database should take into account the kinds of queries that are likely to be asked and the dependencies that exist among the attributes, but the small databases for which *q* is likely to be fast enough, with only a few tables, are unlikely to uncover subtleties in `relfile` design.

q, an awk-like query language

Our query language *q* consists of single-line awk programs with attribute names in place of field names. The query processor `qawk` answers a query as follows:

1. It determines the set of attributes in the query.

2. Starting from the beginning of the `relfile`, it finds the first table whose attributes include all the attributes in the query. If this table is a base table, it uses that table as the input for the query. If the table is a derived table, it constructs the derived table and uses it as the input. (This means that every combination of attributes that might appear in a query must also appear in either a base or derived table in the `relfile`.)

3. It transforms the *q* query into an awk program by replacing the symbolic field references by the appropriate numeric field references. This program is then applied to the table determined in step (2).

The *q* query

```
$continent ~ /Asia/ { print $country, $population }
```

mentions the attributes `continent`, `country`, and `population`, all of which are included in the attributes of the first table `countries`. The query processor translates this query into the program

```
$4 ~ /Asia/  { print $1, $3 }
```

which it applies to the `countries` file.

The *q* query

```
{ print $country, $population, $capital }
```

contains the attributes `country`, `population`, and `capital`, all of which are included only in the derived table `cc`. The query processor therefore constructs the derived table `cc` using the commands listed in the `relfile` and translates this query into the program

```
{ print $1, $3, $5 }
```

which it applies to the freshly constructed cc file.

We have been using the word "query," but it's certainly possible to use qawk to compute as well, as in this computation of the average area:

```
{ area += $area }; END { print area/NR }
```

qawk, a q-to-awk translator

We conclude this chapter with the implementation of qawk, the processor that translates q queries into awk programs.

First, qawk reads the relfile and collects the table names into the array relname. It collects any commands needed to construct the i-th table and stores them into the array cmd beginning at location cmd[i,1]. It also collects the attributes of each table into the two-dimensional array attr; the entry attr[i,a] holds the index of the attribute named a in the i-th table.

Second, qawk reads a query and determines which attributes it uses; these are all the strings of the form $name in the query. Using the subset function, it determines T_i, the first table whose attributes include all of the attributes present in the query. It substitutes the indexes of these attributes into the original query to generate an awk program, issues whatever commands are needed to create T_i, then executes the newly generated awk program with T_i as input.

The second step is repeated for each subsequent query. The following diagram outlines the behavior of qawk:

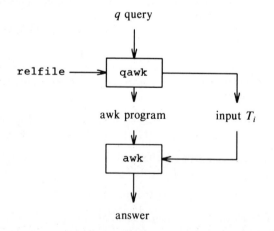

Here is the implementation of qawk:

```
# qawk - awk relational database query processor

BEGIN { readrel("relfile") }
/./   { doquery($0) }

function readrel(f) {
    while (getline <f > 0)   # parse relfile
        if ($0 ~ /^[A-Za-z]+ *:/) {      # name:
            gsub(/[^A-Za-z]+/, "", $0)  # remove all but name
            relname[++nrel] = $0
        } else if ($0 ~ /^[ \t]*!/)       # !command...
            cmd[nrel, ++ncmd[nrel]] = substr($0,index($0,"!")+1)
        else if ($0 ~ /^[ \t]*[A-Za-z]+[ \t]*$/)   # attribute
            attr[nrel, $1] = ++nattr[nrel]
        else if ($0 !~ /^[ \t]*$/)          # not white space
            print "bad line in relfile:", $0
}
function doquery(s,   i,j) {
    for (i in qattr)  # clean up for next query
        delete qattr[i]
    query = s      # put $names in query into qattr, without $
    while (match(s, /\$[A-Za-z]+/)) {
        qattr[substr(s, RSTART+1, RLENGTH-1)] = 1
        s = substr(s, RSTART+RLENGTH+1)
    }
    for (i = 1; i <= nrel && !subset(qattr, attr, i); )
        i++
    if (i > nrel)     # didn't find a table with all attributes
        missing(qattr)
    else {            # table i contains attributes in query
        for (j in qattr)   # create awk program
            gsub("\\$" j, "$" attr[i,j], query)
        for (j = 1; j <= ncmd[i]; j++)  # create table i
            if (system(cmd[i, j]) != 0) {
                print "command failed, query skipped\n", cmd[i,j]
                return
            }
        awkcmd = sprintf("awk -F'\t' '%s' %s", query, relname[i])
        printf("query: %s\n", awkcmd)    # for debugging
        system(awkcmd)
    }
}
function subset(q, a, r,   i) {  # is q a subset of a[r]?
    for (i in q)
        if (!((r,i) in a))
            return 0
    return 1
}
function missing(x,    i) {
    print "no table contains all of the following attributes:"
    for (i in x)
        print i
}
```

Exercise 4-9. If your operating system doesn't support awk's system function, modify qawk to write the appropriate sequence of commands in a file or files that can be executed separately. □

Exercise 4-10. As it constructs a derived table, qawk calls system once for each command. Modify qawk to collect all of the commands for building a table into one string and to execute them with a single call to system. □

Exercise 4-11. Modify qawk to check whether a derived file that is going to be used as input has already been computed. If this file has been computed and the base files from which it was derived have not been modified since, then we can use the derived file without recomputing it. Look at the program make presented in Chapter 7. □

Exercise 4-12. Provide a way to enter and edit multiline queries. Multiline queries can be collected with minimal changes to qawk. One possibility for editing is a way to invoke your favorite text editor; another is to write a very simple editor in awk itself. □

4.4 Summary

In this chapter we have tried to illustrate how to use awk to access and print information in an organized fashion, in contrast to the more typical *ad hoc* uses of Chapter 3.

For generating reports, a "divide-and-conquer" strategy is often best: prepare the data in one program, sort if necessary, then format with a second program. Control breaks can be handled either by looking behind, or, often more elegantly, by an input pushback mechanism. (They can also sometimes be done by a pipeline too, although we didn't show that in this chapter.) For the details of formatting, a good alternative to counting characters by hand is to use some program that does all the mechanical parts.

Although awk is not a tool for production databases, it is quite reasonable for small personal databases, and it also serves well for illustrating some of the fundamental notions. The qawk processor is an attempt to demonstrate both of these aspects.

Bibliographic Notes

There are many good books on databases; you might try J. D. Ullman's *Principles of Database Systems* (Computer Science Press, 1986).

5   PROCESSING WORDS

The programs in this chapter share a common theme: the manipulation of text. The examples include programs that generate random words and sentences, that carry on limited dialogues with the user, and that do text processing. Most are toys, of value mainly as illustrations, but some of the document preparation programs are in regular use.

5.1   Random Text Generation

Programs that generate random data have many uses. Such programs can be created using the built-in function rand, which returns a pseudo-random number each time it is called. The rand function starts generating random numbers from the same seed each time a program using it is invoked, so if you want a different sequence each time, you must call srand() once, which will initialize rand with a seed computed from the current time.

Random Choices

Each time it is called, rand returns a random floating point number greater than or equal to 0 and less than 1, but often what is wanted is a random integer between 1 and n. That's easy to compute from rand:

```
# randint - return random integer x, 1 <= x <= n

function randint(n) {
    return int(n * rand()) + 1
}
```

randint(n) scales the floating point number produced by rand so it is at least 0 and less than n, truncates the fractional part to make an integer between 0 and n-1, then adds 1.

We can use randint to select random letters like this:

```
# randlet - generate random lower-case letter

function randlet() {
    return substr("abcdefghijklmnopqrstuvwxyz", randint(26), 1)
}
```

Using `randint`, it's also easy to print a single random element from an array of n items `x[1]`, `x[2]`, ..., `x[n]`:

```
    print x[randint(n)]
```

A more interesting problem, however, is to print several random entries from the array *in the original order*. For example, if the elements of **x** are in increasing order, the random sample also has to be in order.

The function `choose` prints **k** random elements in order from the first n elements of an array **A**.

```
    # choose - print in order k random elements from A[1]..A[n]

    function choose(A, k, n,    i) {
        for (i = 1; n > 0; i++)
            if (rand() < k/n--) {
                print A[i]
                k--
            }
    }
```

In the body of the function, **k** is the number of entries that still need to be printed, and n is the number of array elements yet to be examined. The decision whether to print the i-th element is determined by the test `rand() < k/n`; each time an element is printed, **k** is decreased, and each time the test is made, n is decreased.

Exercise 5-1. Test `rand` to see how random its output really is. □

Exercise 5-2. Write a program to generate k distinct random integers between 1 and n in time proportional to k. □

Exercise 5-3. Write a program to generate random bridge hands. □

Cliche Generation

Our next example is a cliche generator, which creates new cliches out of old ones. The input is a set of sentences like

```
    A rolling stone:gathers no moss.
    History:repeats itself.
    He who lives by the sword:shall die by the sword.
    A jack of all trades:is master of none.
    Nature:abhors a vacuum.
    Every man:has a price.
    All's well that:ends well.
```

where a colon separates subject from predicate. Our cliche program combines a random subject with a random predicate; with luck it produces the occasional mildly amusing aphorism:

```
A rolling stone repeats itself.
History abhors a vacuum.
Nature repeats itself.
All's well that gathers no moss.
He who lives by the sword has a price.
```

The code is straightforward:

```
# cliche - generate an endless stream of cliches
#      input:  lines of form subject:predicate
#      output: lines of random subject and random predicate

BEGIN { FS = ":" }
      { x[NR] = $1; y[NR] = $2 }
END   { for (;;) print x[randint(NR)], y[randint(NR)] }

function randint(n) { return int(n * rand()) + 1 }
```

Don't forget that this program is intentionally an infinite loop.

Random Sentences

A *context-free grammar* is a set of rules that defines how to generate or analyze a set of sentences. Each rule, called a *production*, has the form

$$A \rightarrow B\ C\ D \dots$$

The meaning of this production is that any A can be "rewritten" as $B\ C\ D$ .... The symbol on the left-hand side, A, is called a *nonterminal*, because it can be expanded further. The symbols on the right-hand side can be nonterminals (including more A's) or *terminals*, so called because they do *not* get expanded. There can be several rules with the same left side; terminals and nonterminals can be repeated in right sides.

In Chapter 6 we will show a grammar for a part of awk itself, and use that to write a parser that analyzes awk programs. In this chapter, however, our interest is in generation, not analysis. For example, here is a grammar for sentences like "the boy walks slowly" and "the girl runs very very quickly."

```
Sentence -> Nounphrase Verbphrase
Nounphrase -> the boy
Nounphrase -> the girl
Verbphrase -> Verb Modlist Adverb
Verb -> runs
Verb -> walks
Modlist ->
Modlist -> very Modlist
Adverb -> quickly
Adverb -> slowly
```

The productions generate sentences for nonterminals as follows. Suppose
`Sentence` is the starting nonterminal. Choose a production with that nonterminal on the left-hand side:

```
Sentence -> Nounphrase Verbphrase
```

Next pick any nonterminal from the right side, for example, `Nounphrase`, and
rewrite it with any one of the productions for which it is the left side:

```
Sentence -> Nounphrase Verbphrase
         -> the boy Verbphrase
```

Now pick another nonterminal from the resulting right side (this time only
`Verbphrase` remains) and rewrite it by one of its productions:

```
Sentence -> Nounphrase Verbphrase
         -> the boy Verbphrase
         -> the boy Verb Modlist Adverb
```

Continue rewriting this way until no more nonterminals remain:

```
Sentence -> Nounphrase Verbphrase
         -> the boy Verbphrase
         -> the boy Verb Modlist Adverb
         -> the boy walks very Modlist Adverb
         -> the boy walks very Adverb
         -> the boy walks very quickly
```

The result is a sentence for the starting nonterminal. This derivation process is
the opposite of the sentence-diagraming procedure taught in elementary school:
rather than combining an adverb and a verb into a verb phrase, we are expanding a verb phrase into a verb and an adverb.

The productions for `Modlist` are interesting. One rule says to replace
`Modlist` by `very Modlist`; each time we do this, the sentence gets longer.
Fortunately, this potentially infinite process terminates as soon as we replace
`Modlist` by the other possibility, which is the null string.

We will now present a program to generate sentences in a grammar, starting
from any specified nonterminal. The program reads the grammar from a file
and records the number of times each left-hand side occurs, plus the number of
right-hand sides it has, and the components of each. Thereafter, whenever a
nonterminal is typed, a random sentence for that nonterminal is generated.

The data structure created by this program uses three arrays to store the
grammar: `lhs[A]` gives the number of productions for the nonterminal `A`,
`rhscnt[A,i]` gives the number of symbols on the right-hand side of the i-th
production for `A`, and `rhslist[A,i,j]` contains the j-th symbol in the i-th
right-hand side for `A`. For our grammar, these arrays contain:

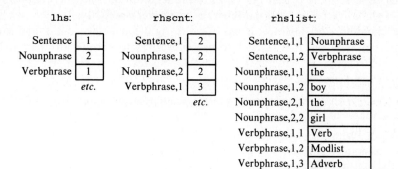

The program itself is this:

```
# sentgen - random sentence generator
#    input:  grammar file; sequence of nonterminals
#    output: a random sentence for each nonterminal

BEGIN {  # read rules from grammar file
    while (getline < "grammar" > 0)
        if ($2 == "->") {
            i = ++lhs[$1]                # count lhs
            rhscnt[$1, i] = NF-2         # how many in rhs
            for (j = 3; j <= NF; j++)    # record them
                rhslist[$1, i, j-2] = $j
        } else
            print "illegal production: " $0
}

{   if ($1 in lhs) {  # nonterminal to expand
        gen($1)
        printf("\n")
    } else
        print "unknown nonterminal: " $0
}

function gen(sym,    i, j) {
    if (sym in lhs) {           # a nonterminal
        i = int(lhs[sym] * rand()) + 1   # random production
        for (j = 1; j <= rhscnt[sym, i]; j++) # expand rhs's
            gen(rhslist[sym, i, j])
    } else
        printf("%s ", sym)
}
```

The function gen("A") generates a sentence for the nonterminal A. It calls itself recursively to expand nonterminals introduced by previous expansions. Remember to make sure that all the temporary variables used by a recursive function appear in the parameter list of the function declaration. If they do not, they are global variables, and the program won't work properly.

We chose to use separate arrays for the right-hand-side counts and components, but it is possible instead to use subscripts to encode different fields, rather like records or structures in other languages. For example, the array `rhscnt[i,j]` could be part of `rhslist`, as `rhslist[i,j,"cnt"]`.

Exercise 5-4. Write a grammar for generating plausible-sounding text from a field that appeals to you — business, politics, and computing are all good possibilities. □

Exercise 5-5. With some grammars, there is an unacceptably high probability that the sentence-generation program will go into a derivation that just keeps getting longer. Add a mechanism to limit the length of a derivation. □

Exercise 5-6. Add probabilities to the rules of a grammar, so that some of the rules associated with a nonterminal are more likely to be chosen than others. □

Exercise 5-7. Implement a nonrecursive version of the sentence-generation program. □

5.2   Interactive Text-Manipulation

It is easy to write interactive programs in awk. We'll illustrate the basic ideas with two programs. The first tests arithmetic skills, and the second tests knowledge of particular subject areas.

Skills Testing: Arithmetic

The following program `arith` (best suited for a very young child) presents a sequence of addition problems like

```
7 + 9 = ?
```

After each problem, the user types an answer. If the answer is right, the user is praised and presented with another problem. If the answer is wrong, the program asks for the answer again. If the user provides no answer at all, the right answer is printed before the next problem is presented.

The program is invoked with one of two command lines:

```
awk -f arith
awk -f arith n
```

If there is an argument after `arith` on the command line, the argument is used to limit the maximum size of the numbers in each problem. After this argument has been read, `ARGV[1]` is reset to `"-"` so the program will be able to read the answers from the standard input. If no argument is specified, the maximum size will be 10.

```
# arith - addition drill
#    usage:  awk -f arith [ optional problem size ]
#    output: queries of the form "i + j = ?"

BEGIN {
    maxnum = ARGC > 1 ? ARGV[1] : 10    # default size is 10
    ARGV[1] = "-"   # read standard input subsequently
    srand()         # reset rand from time of day
    do {
        n1 = randint(maxnum)
        n2 = randint(maxnum)
        printf("%g + %g = ? ", n1, n2)
        while ((input = getline) > 0)
            if ($0 == n1 + n2) {
                print "Right!"
                break
            } else if ($0 == "") {
                print n1 + n2
                break
            } else
                printf("wrong, try again: ")
    } while (input > 0)
}

function randint(n) { return int(rand()*n)+1 }
```

Exercise 5-8. Add the other arithmetic operators. Add a way to provide hints for wrong answers. □

Skills Testing: Quiz

Our second example is a program called quiz that asks questions from some specified file of questions and answers. For example, consider testing knowledge of chemical elements. Suppose the question-and-answer file quiz.elems contains the symbol, atomic number, and full name for each element, separated by colons. The first line identifies the fields of subsequent lines:

```
symbol:number:name¦element
H:1:Hydrogen
He:2:Helium
Li:3:Lithium
Be:4:Beryllium
B:5:Boron
C:6:Carbon
N:7:Nitrogen
O:8:Oxygen
F:9:Fluorine
Ne:10:Neon
Na:11:Sodium¦Natrium
...
```

The program uses the first line to decide which field is the question and which is the answer, then reads the rest of the file into an array, from which it presents random items and checks answers. After typing the command line

```
awk -f quiz quiz.elems name symbol
```

we might engage in a dialogue like this:

```
Beryllium? B
wrong, try again: Be
Right!
Fluorine?
...
```

Notice that alternative answers (for example, sodium or natrium) are easily handled with regular expressions in the data file.

```
# quiz - present a quiz
#    usage: awk -f quiz topicfile question-subj answer-subj

BEGIN {
    FS = ":"
    if (ARGC != 4)
        error("usage: awk -f quiz topicfile question answer")
    if (getline <ARGV[1] < 0)      # 1st line is subj:subj:...
        error("no such quiz as " ARGV[1])
    for (q = 1; q <= NF; q++)
        if ($q ~ ARGV[2])
            break
    for (a = 1; a <= NF; a++)
        if ($a ~ ARGV[3])
            break
    if (q > NF || a > NF || q == a)
        error("valid subjects are " $0)
    while (getline <ARGV[1] > 0) # load the quiz
        qa[++nq] = $0
    ARGC = 2; ARGV[1] = "-"         # now read standard input
    srand()
    do {
        split(qa[int(rand()*nq + 1)], x)
        printf("%s? ", x[q])
        while ((input = getline) > 0)
            if ($0 ~ "^(" x[a] ")$") {
                print "Right!"
                break
            } else if ($0 == "") {
                print x[a]
                break
            } else
                printf("wrong, try again: ")
    } while (input > 0)
}

function error(s) { printf("error: %s\n", s); exit }
```

We have to surround the regular expression for the right answer with ^ and $; without this, any matching substring of the right answer would also be accepted (so N would match Ne and Na as well as N).

Exercise 5-9. Modify quiz so that it does not present any question more than once. □

5.3 Text Processing

Because of its string manipulation capabilities, awk is useful for tasks that arise in text processing and document preparation. As examples, this section contains programs for counting words, formatting text, maintaining cross-references, making KWIC indexes, and preparing indexes.

Word Counts

In Chapter 1, we presented a program to count the number of lines, words, and characters in a file, where a word was defined as any contiguous sequence of nonblank, nontab characters. A related problem is to count the number of times each different word appears in a document. One way to solve this problem is to isolate the words, sort them to bring identical words together, and then count occurrences of each word with a control-break program.

Another way, well suited to awk, is to isolate the words and aggregate the count for each word in an associative array. To do this properly, we have to decide what a word really is. In the following program, a word is a field with the punctuation removed, so that, for example, "word" and "word;" and "(word)" are all counted in the entry for word. The END action prints the word frequencies, sorted in decreasing order.

```
# wordfreq - print number of occurrences of each word
#    input:  text
#    output: number-word pairs sorted by number

    { gsub(/[.,:;!?(){}]/, "")     # remove punctuation
      for (i = 1; i <= NF; i++)
          count[$i]++
    }
END { for (w in count)
          print count[w], w | "sort -rn"
    }
```

The top ten words for a draft of this chapter:

312 the	152 a	126 of	121 is	110 to
92 and	72 in	71 The	59 at	54 that

Exercise 5-10. Modify the word-counting program to fold upper and lower case together, so that the and The are counted together. □

Exercise 5-11. Write a program to count the number of sentences in a document and their lengths. □

Exercise 5-12. Write the control-break program to count words. How does its performance compare with `wordfreq`? □

Text Formatting

The program `fmt` formats its input into lines that are at most 60 characters long, by moving words to fill each line as much as possible. Blank lines cause paragraph breaks; otherwise, there are no commands. It's useful for formatting text that was originally created without thought to line length.

```
# fmt - format
#     input:  text
#     output: text formatted into lines of <= 60 characters

/./   { for (i = 1; i <= NF; i++) addword($i) }
/^$/  { printline(); print "" }
END   { printline() }

function addword(w) {
    if (length(line) + length(w) > 60)
        printline()
    line = line " " w
}

function printline() {
    if (length(line) > 0) {
        print substr(line, 2)    # removes leading blank
        line = ""
    }
}
```

Exercise 5-13. Modify `fmt` to align the right margin of the text it prints. □

Exercise 5-14. Enhance `fmt` to infer the proper format of a document by recognizing probable titles, headings, lists, etc. Rather than formatting, it could generate formatting commands for a formatter like `troff` or TEX. □

Maintaining Cross-References in Manuscripts

A common problem in document preparation is creating a consistent set of names or numbers for items like bibliographic citations, figures, tables, examples, and so on. Some text formatters help out with this task, but most expect you to do it yourself. Our next example is a technique for numbering cross-references. It's quite useful for documents like technical papers or books.

As the document is being written, the author creates and uses symbolic names for the various items that will be cross-referenced. Because the names are symbolic, items can be added, deleted, and rearranged without having to change any existing names. Two programs create the version in which the symbolic names are replaced by suitable numbers. Here is a sample document containing symbolic names for two bibliographic citations and one figure:

```
.#Fig _quotes_
Figure _quotes_ gives two brief quotations from famous books.
```

```
                    Figure _quotes_:
```

```
.#Bib _alice_
   "... `and what is the use of a book,' thought Alice,
   `without pictures or conversations?'" [_alice_]
```

```
.#Bib _huck_
   "... if I'd a knowed what a trouble it was to make a book
   I wouldn't a tackled it and ain't agoing to no more." [_huck_]
```

```
[_alice_] Carroll, L., Alice's Adventures in Wonderland,
    Macmillan, 1865.
[_huck_] Twain, M., Adventures of Huckleberry Finn,
    Webster & Co., 1885.
```

Each symbolic name is defined by a line of the form

```
.#Category _SymbolicName_
```

Such a definition can appear anywhere in the document, and there can be as many different categories as the author wants. Throughout the document an item is referred to by its symbolic name. We have chosen symbolic names that begin and end with an underscore, but any names can be used as long as they can be separated from other text. (Item names must all be distinct, even if in different categories.) The names .#Fig and .#Bib begin with a period so they will be ignored by the troff formatter in case the document is printed without resolving the cross-references; with a different formatter, a different convention may be required.

The conversion creates a new version of the document in which the definitions are removed and each symbolic name is replaced by a number. In each category the numbers start at one and go up sequentially in the order in which the definitions for that category appear in the original document.

The conversion is done by passing the document through two programs. This division of labor is another instance of a powerful general technique: the first program creates a second program to do the rest of the job. In this case, the first program, called xref, scans the document and creates the second program, called xref.temp, that does the actual conversion. If the original version of the manuscript is in the file document, the version with the numeric references is created by typing:

```
awk -f xref document >xref.temp
awk -f xref.temp document
```

The output of the second program can be directed to a printer or text formatter.

The result for our sample above:

```
Figure 1 gives two brief quotations from famous books.

                       Figure 1:

  "... `and what is the use of a book,' thought Alice,
  `without pictures or conversations?'" [1]

  "... if I'd a knowed what a trouble it was to make a book
  I wouldn't a tackled it and ain't agoing to no more." [2]


  [1] Carroll, L., Alice's Adventures in Wonderland,
      Macmillan, 1865.
  [2] Twain, M., Adventures of Huckleberry Finn,
      Webster & Co., 1885.
```

The xref program searches the document for lines beginning with ".#"; for each such definition it increments a counter in the array count for items of that category and prints a gsub statement.

```
# xref - create numeric values for symbolic names
#     input:  text with definitions for symbolic names
#     output: awk program to replace symbolic names by numbers

/^\.#/ { printf("{ gsub(/%s/, \"%d\") }\n", $2, ++count[$1]) }
END    { printf("!/^[.]#/\n") }
```

The output of xref on the file above is the second program, xref.temp:

```
{ gsub(/_quotes_/, "1") }
{ gsub(/_alice_/, "1") }
{ gsub(/_huck_/, "2") }
!/^[.]#/
```

The gsub's globally substitute numbers for the symbolic names; the last statement deletes the definitions by not printing lines that begin with .#.

Exercise 5-15. What might happen if the trailing underscore were omitted from a symbolic name? □

Exercise 5-16. Modify xref to detect multiple definitions of a symbolic name. □

Exercise 5-17. Modify xref to create editing commands for your favorite text or stream editor (e.g., sed) instead of creating awk commands. What effect does this have on performance? □

Exercise 5-18. How could you modify xref to make only a single pass over the input? What restrictions on placement of definitions does this imply? □

Making a KWIC Index

A Keyword-In-Context or KWIC index is an index that shows each word in the context of the line it is found in; it provides essentially the same information as a concordance, although in a different format. Consider the three sentences

```
All's well that ends well.
Nature abhors a vacuum.
Every man has a price.
```

Here is a KWIC index for these sentences:

```
    Every man has  a price.
    Nature abhors  a vacuum.
           Nature  abhors a vacuum.
                   All's well that ends well.
  All's well that  ends well.
                   Every man has a price.
       Every man  has a price.
           Every  man has a price.
                   Nature abhors a vacuum.
   Every man has a  price.
      All's well  that ends well.
  Nature abhors a  vacuum.
           All's  well that ends well.
All's well that ends  well.
```

The problem of constructing a KWIC index has an interesting history in the field of software engineering. It was proposed as a design exercise by Parnas in 1972; he presented a solution based on a single program. The Unix command ptx, which does the same job in much the same way, is about 500 lines of C.

The convenience of Unix pipelines suggests a three-step solution: a first program generates rotations of each input line so that each word in turn is at the front, a sort puts them in order, and another program unrotates. This forms the basis of the version in *Software Tools*, which required about 70 lines of Ratfor (a structured Fortran dialect), excluding the sort.

This method is even easier with awk; it can be done by a pair of short awk programs with a sort between them:

```
awk '
# kwic - generate kwic index

{   print $0
    for (i = length($0); i > 0; i--) # compute length only once
        if (substr($0,i,1) == " ")
            # prefix space suffix ==> suffix tab prefix
            print substr($0,i+1) "\t" substr($0,1,i-1)
} ' |
sort -f |
awk '
BEGIN { FS = "\t"; WID = 30 }
      { printf("%" WID "s  %s\n", substr($2,length($2)-WID+1),
            substr($1,1,WID)) }
' 
```

The first program prints a copy of each input line. It also prints an output line for every blank within each input line; the output consists of the part of the input line after the blank, followed by a tab, followed by the part before the blank.

All output lines are then piped into the Unix command `sort -f` which sorts them, "folding" upper and lower-case letters together, so that, for example, `Jack` and `jack` will appear adjacent.

From the output of the `sort` command, the second awk program reconstructs the input lines, appropriately formatted. It prints a portion of the part after the tab, followed by a blank, followed by a portion of the part in front of the tab.

Exercise 5-19. Add a "stop list" to `kwic`: a set of words like "a" and "the" that are not to be taken as keywords. □

Exercise 5-20. Fix `kwic` to show as much as possible of lines, by wrapping around at the ends rather than truncating. □

Exercise 5-21. Write a program to make a concordance instead of a KWIC index: for each significant word, show all the sentences or phrases where the word appears. □

Making Indexes

One task that accompanies writing a major document like a book or a manual is preparing an index. There are two parts to this job. The first is deciding on the terms to be indexed; this is demanding intellectual work if done well, and not very susceptible to mechanization. The other part really is mechanical: producing, from a list of index terms and page numbers, a properly alphabetized and formatted index, like the one at the back of this book.

In the remainder of this section, we are going to use awk and the `sort` command to build the core of an indexer (whose slightly bigger sibling was used to create the index of this book). The basic idea is similar to what was used in the KWIC index program: divide and conquer. The job is broken down into a sequence of easy pieces, each based on a one-line sort or a short awk program. Since the pieces are tiny and separate, they can be adapted or augmented with others quite easily, to satisfy more complicated indexing requirements.

These programs contain a number of details that are specific to the `troff` formatter, which we used to typeset this book. These details would change if the programs were to be used with another formatter, such as TEX or Scribe, but the basic structure will be the same.

We indexed the book by inserting formatting commands into the text. When the text is run through `troff`, these commands cause index terms and page numbers to be collected in a file. This produces a sequence of lines like the following, which is the raw material for the index-preparation programs (a single tab separates the number from the index term):

```
[FS] variable             35
[FS] variable             36
arithmetic operators      36
coercion rules            44
string comparison         44
numeric comparison        44
arithmetic operators      44
coercion~to number        45
coercion~to string        45
[if]-[else] statement     47
control-flow statements   48
[FS] variable             52
...
```

The intent is that an index term like

```
    string comparison         44
```

should ultimately appear in the index in two forms:

```
    string comparison  44
    comparison, string  44
```

Index terms are normally split and rotated at each blank in the term. The tilde ~ is used to prevent splitting:

```
    coercion~to number        45
```

is not to be indexed under "to."

There are a couple of other frills. Since we use troff, some troff size- and font-change commands are recognized and properly ignored during sorting. Furthermore, because font changes occur frequently in the index, we use the shorthand [...] to indicate material that should appear in the index in the constant-width font; for example

```
    [if]-[else] statement
```

is to be printed as

```
    if-else statement
```

The indexing process is a composition of six commands:

ix.sort1	sort input by index term, then by page number
ix.collapse	collapse number lists for identical terms
ix.rotate	generate rotations of index term
ix.genkey	generate a sort key to force proper ordering
ix.sort2	sort by sort key
ix.format	generate final output

These commands gradually massage the index-term, page-number pairs into the final form of the index. For the remainder of this section we will consider these commands in order.

The initial sort takes the index-term, page-number pairs as input and brings identical terms together in page-number order:

```
# ix.sort1 - sort by index term, then by page number
#     input/output: lines of the form string tab number
#     sort by string, then by number; discard duplicates

sort -t'tab' +0 -1 +1n -2 -u
```

The arguments to the sort command need explanation: -t'*tab*' says tab is
the field separator; +0 -1 says the first sort key is field 1, which is to be sorted
alphabetically; +1n -2 says the second sort key is field 2, which is to be sorted
numerically; and -u says to discard duplicates. (In Chapter 6, we describe a
sort-generator program that will create these arguments for you.) The output of
ix.sort1 on the input above is:

```
[FS] variable               35
[FS] variable               36
[FS] variable               52
[if]-[else] statement       47
arithmetic operators        36
arithmetic operators        44
coercion rules              44
coercion-to number          45
coercion-to string          45
control-flow statements     48
numeric comparison          44
string comparison           44
```

This output becomes the input to the next program, ix.collapse, which
puts the page numbers for identical terms on a single line, using a variation of
the usual control-break program.

```
# ix.collapse - combine number lists for identical terms
#     input:  string tab num \n string tab num ...
#     output: string tab num num ...

BEGIN { FS = OFS = "\t" }
$1 != prev {
    if (NR > 1)
        printf("\n")
    prev = $1
    printf("%s\t%s", $1, $2)
    next
}
    { printf(" %s", $2) }

END { if (NR > 1) printf("\n") }
```

The output of ix.collapse is

```
[FS] variable               35  36  52
[if]-[else] statement       47
arithmetic operators        36  44
coercion rules              44
coercion~to number          45
coercion~to string          45
control-flow statements     48
numeric comparison          44
string comparison           44
```

The next program, `ix.rotate`, produces rotations of the index terms from this output, for example generating "`comparison, string`" from "`string comparison.`" This is much the same computation as in the KWIC index, although we've written it differently. Notice the assignment expression in the `for` loop.

```
# ix.rotate - generate rotations of index terms
#    input:  string tab num num ...
#    output: rotations of string tab num num ...

BEGIN { FS = OFS = "\t" }
{    print $1, $2    # unrotated form
     for (i = 1; (j = index(substr($1, i+1), " ")) > 0; ) {
          i += j         # find each blank, rotate around it
          printf("%s, %s\t%s\n",
               substr($1, i+1), substr($1, 1, i-1), $2)
     }
}
```

The output from `ix.rotate` begins

```
[FS] variable               35  36  52
variable, [FS]              35  36  52
[if]-[else] statement       47
statement, [if]-[else]      47
arithmetic operators        36  44
operators, arithmetic       36  44
coercion rules              44
rules, coercion             44
coercion~to number          45
number, coercion~to         45
coercion~to string          45
...
```

The next stage is to sort these rotated index terms. The problem with sorting them directly is that there may still be embedded formatting information like [...] that will interfere with the sort order. So each line is prefixed with a key that assures the proper order; the key will be stripped off later. The program `ix.genkey` creates the key from the index term by removing `troff` size and font change commands, which look like \s+*n*, or \s-*n*, or \f*x*, or \f(*xx*. It also converts the tildes to blanks, and removes any nonalphanumeric characters other than blank from the sort key.

```
# ix.genkey - generate sort key to force ordering
#    input:  string tab num num ...
#    output: sort key tab string tab num num ...

BEGIN { FS = OFS = "\t" }

{   gsub(/~/, " ", $1)          # tildes now become blanks
    key = $1
    # remove troff size and font change commands from key
    gsub(/\\f.¦\\f\(..¦\\s[-+][0-9]/, "", key)
    # keep blanks, letters, digits only
    gsub(/[^a-zA-Z0-9 ]+/, "", key)
    if (key ~ /^[^a-zA-Z]/)     # force nonalpha to sort first
        key = " " key           # by prefixing a blank
    print key, $1, $2
}
```

The output is now

```
FS variable             [FS] variable           35 36 52
variable FS             variable, [FS]          35 36 52
ifelse statement        [if]-[else] statement   47
statement ifelse        statement, [if]-[else]  47
arithmetic operators    arithmetic operators    36 44
operators arithmetic    operators, arithmetic   36 44
coercion rules          coercion rules          44
rules coercion          rules, coercion         44
coercion to number      coercion to number      45
...
```

The first few lines should clarify the distinction between the sort key and the actual data.

The second sort puts terms into alphabetical order; as before, the -f option folds upper and lower case together, and -d is dictionary order.

```
# ix.sort2 - sort by sort key
#      input/output: sort-key tab string tab num num ...

sort -f -d
```

This puts items into their final order:

```
arithmetic operators    arithmetic operators    36 44
coercion rules          coercion rules          44
coercion to number      coercion to number      45
coercion to string      coercion to string      45
comparison numeric      comparison, numeric     44
comparison string       comparison, string      44
controlflow statements  control-flow statements 48
FS variable             [FS] variable           35 36 52
ifelse statement        [if]-[else] statement   47
number coercion to      number, coercion to     45
...
```

The last stage, `ix.format`, removes the sort key, expands any [...] into `troff` font-change commands, and precedes each term by a formatting command `.XX` that can be used by a text formatter to control size, position, etc. (The actual command sequences are quite specific to `troff`; you can safely ignore the details.)

```
# ix.format - remove key, restore size and font commands
#    input:  sort key tab string tab num num ...
#    output: troff format, ready to print

BEGIN { FS = "\t" }

{    gsub(/ /, ", ", $3)          # commas between page numbers
     gsub(/\[/, "\\f(CW", $2)     # set constant-width font
     gsub(/\]/, "\\fP", $2)       # restore previous font
     print ".XX"                  # user-definable command
     printf("%s  %s\n", $2, $3)   # actual index entry
}
```

The final output begins like this:

```
.XX
arithmetic operators   36, 44
.XX
coercion rules   44
.XX
coercion to number   45
...
```

To recapitulate, the indexing process consists of a pipeline of six commands

```
sh ix.sort1 |
awk -f ix.collapse |
awk -f ix.rotate |
awk -f ix.genkey |
sh ix.sort2 |
awk -f ix.format
```

If these are applied to the input of index-term, page-number pairs at the beginning of this section, and formatted, the result looks like this:

```
arithmetic operators  36, 44
coercion rules  44
coercion to number  45
coercion to string  45
comparison, numeric  44
comparison, string  44
control-flow statements  48
FS variable  35, 36, 52
if-else statement  47
number, coercion to  45
numeric comparison  44
```

Many enhancements and variations are possible; some of the most useful are suggested in the exercises. The important lesson, however, is that dividing the job into a sequence of tiny programs makes the whole task quite simple, and also makes it easy to adapt to new requirements.

Exercise 5-22. Modify or augment the indexing programs to provide hierarchical indexes, *See* and *See also* terms, and Roman-numeral page numbers. □

Exercise 5-23. Allow literal [,], ~, and % characters in index terms. □

Exercise 5-24. Attack the problem of creating an index automatically by building tools that prepare lists of words, phrases, etc. How well does the list of word frequencies produced by `wordfreq` suggest index terms or topics? □

5.4 Summary

Awk programs can manipulate text with much the same ease that languages like C or Pascal manipulate numbers — storage is managed automatically, and the built-in operators and functions provide many of the necessary services. As a result, awk is usually good for prototyping, and sometimes it is quite adequate for production use. The indexing programs are a good example — we used a version of them to index this book.

Bibliographic Notes

Our quiz program is modeled after the Unix version, originally created by Doug McIlroy. The idea for the cliche generator comes from Ron Hardin. Parnas' paper on KWIC indexes, "On the criteria to be used in decomposing systems into modules," appeared in *Communications of the ACM*, December, 1972. Jon Bentley provided early versions of the KWIC index program, described in *Programming Pearls* in *Communications of the ACM*, June, 1985. The program for maintaining cross-references is based on Aho and Sethi, "Maintaining Cross-References in Manuscripts," CSTR 127, AT&T Bell Laboratories, Murray Hill, NJ (1986). The programs for constructing indexes are derived from Bentley and Kernighan, "Tools for Printing Indexes," CSTR 128, AT&T Bell Laboratories, Murray Hill, NJ (1986).

6 LITTLE LANGUAGES

Awk is often used to develop translators for "little languages," that is, languages for specialized applications. One reason for writing a translator is to learn how a language processor works. The first example in this chapter is an assembler that in twenty lines or so shows the essentials of the assembly process. It is accompanied by an interpreter that executes the assembled programs. The combination illustrates the rudiments of assembly language and machine architecture. Other examples show the basic operation of a postfix calculator and of a recursive-descent translator for a subset of awk itself.

Another reason may be to experiment with the syntax or semantics of a special-purpose language before making a large investment in implementation. As examples, this chapter describes languages for drawing graphs and for specifying sort commands.

A third purpose may be to make a language for practical use, such as one of the calculators in this chapter.

Language processors are built around this conceptual model:

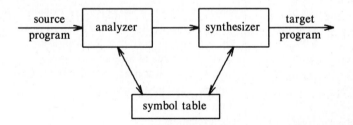

The front end, the analyzer, reads the source program and breaks it apart into its lexical units: operators, operands, and so on. It parses the source program to check that it is grammatically correct, and if it is not, issues the appropriate error messages. Finally, it translates the source program into some intermediate representation from which the back end, the synthesizer, generates the target program. The symbol table communicates information collected by the analyzer about the source program to the synthesizer, which uses it during code generation. Although we have described language processing as a sequence of clearly

131

distinguishable phases, in practice the boundaries are often blurred and the phases may be combined.

Awk is useful for creating processors for experimental languages because its basic operations support many of the tasks involved in language translation. Analysis can often be handled with field splitting and regular expression pattern matching. Symbol tables can be managed with associative arrays. Code generation can be done with `printf` statements.

In this chapter we will develop several translators to illustrate these points. In each case, we will do the minimum that will make the point or teach the lesson; embellishments and refinements are left as exercises.

6.1   An Assembler and Interpreter

Our first example of a language processor is an assembler for a hypothetical computer of the sort often encountered in an introductory course on computer architecture or systems programming. The computer has a single accumulator, ten instructions, and a word-addressable memory of 1000 words. We'll assume that a "word" of machine memory holds five decimal digits; if the word is an instruction, the first two digits encode the operation and the last three digits are the address. The assembly-language instructions are shown in Table 6-1.

TABLE 6-1. ASSEMBLY-LANGUAGE INSTRUCTIONS

OPCODE	INSTRUCTION	MEANING
01	get	read a number from the input into the accumulator
02	put	write the contents of the accumulator to the output
03	ld M	load accumulator with contents of memory location M
04	st M	store contents of accumulator in location M
05	add M	add contents of location M to accumulator
06	sub M	subtract contents of location M from accumulator
07	jpos M	jump to location M if accumulator is positive
08	jz M	jump to location M is accumulator is zero
09	j M	jump to location M
10	halt	stop execution
	const C	assembler pseudo-operation to define a constant C

An assembly-language program is a sequence of statements, each consisting of three fields: label, operation, and operand. Any field may be empty; labels must begin in column one. A program may also contain comments like those in awk programs. Here is a sample assembly-language program that prints the sum of a sequence of integers; the end of the input is marked by a zero.

```
# print sum of input numbers (terminated by zero)

        ld      zero    # initialize sum to zero
        st      sum
loop get                # read a number
        jz      done    # no more input if number is zero
        add     sum     # add in accumulated sum
        st      sum     # store new value back in sum
        j       loop    # go back and read another number

done ld         sum     # print sum
        put
        halt

zero const 0
sum  const
```

The target program resulting from translating this program into machine language is a sequence of integers that represents the contents of memory when the target program is ready to be run. For this program, memory looks like this:

```
 0:  03010          ld    zero    # initialize sum to zero
 1:  04011          st    sum
 2:  01000   loop get             # read a number
 3:  08007          jz    done    # no more input if number is zero
 4:  05011          add   sum     # add in accumulated sum
 5:  04011          st    sum     # store new value back in sum
 6:  09002          j     loop    # go back and read another number
 7:  03011   done ld     sum     # print sum
 8:  02000          put
 9:  10000          halt
10:  00000   zero const 0
11:  00000   sum  const
```

The first field is the memory location; the second is the encoded instruction. Memory location 0 contains the translation of the first instruction of the assembly-language program, ld zero.

The assembler does its translation in two passes. Pass 1 uses field splitting to do lexical and syntactic analysis. It reads the assembly-language program, discards comments, assigns a memory location to each label, and writes an intermediate representation of operations and operands into a temporary file. Pass 2 reads the temporary file, converts symbolic operands to the memory locations computed by pass 1, encodes the operations and operands, and puts the resulting machine-language program into the array mem.

As the other half of the job, we'll build an interpreter that simulates the behavior of the computer on machine-language programs. The interpreter is a loop that fetches an instruction from mem, decodes it into an operator and an operand, and then simulates the instruction. The program counter is kept in the variable pc.

```
# asm - assembler and interpreter for simple computer
#    usage: awk -f asm program-file data-files...

BEGIN {
    srcfile = ARGV[1]
    ARGV[1] = ""   # remaining files are data
    tempfile = "asm.temp"
    n = split("const get put ld st add sub jpos jz j halt", x)
    for (i = 1; i <= n; i++)    # create table of op codes
        op[x[i]] = i-1
}

# ASSEMBLER PASS 1
    FS = "[ \t]+"
    while (getline <srcfile > 0) {
        sub(/#.*/, "")              # strip comments
        symtab[$1] = nextmem    # remember label location
        if ($2 != "") {             # save op, addr if present
            print $2 "\t" $3 >tempfile
            nextmem++
        }
    }
    close(tempfile)

# ASSEMBLER PASS 2
    nextmem = 0
    while (getline <tempfile > 0) {
        if ($2 !~ /^[0-9]*$/)   # if symbolic addr,
            $2 = symtab[$2]     # replace by numeric value
        mem[nextmem++] = 1000 * op[$1] + $2   # pack into word
    }

# INTERPRETER
    for (pc = 0; pc >= 0; ) {
        addr = mem[pc] % 1000
        code = int(mem[pc++] / 1000)
        if      (code == op["get"])  { getline acc }
        else if (code == op["put"])  { print acc }
        else if (code == op["st"])   { mem[addr] = acc }
        else if (code == op["ld"])   { acc  = mem[addr] }
        else if (code == op["add"])  { acc += mem[addr] }
        else if (code == op["sub"])  { acc -= mem[addr] }
        else if (code == op["jpos"]) { if (acc >  0) pc = addr }
        else if (code == op["jz"])   { if (acc == 0) pc = addr }
        else if (code == op["j"])    { pc = addr }
        else if (code == op["halt"]) { pc = -1 }
        else                         { pc = -1 }
    }
}
```

The associative array symtab records memory locations for labels. If there is no label for an input line, symtab[""] is set.

Labels start in column one; operators are preceded by white space. Pass 1 sets the field separator variable FS to the regular expression [\t]+. This causes every maximal sequence of blanks and tabs in the current input line to be a field separator. In particular, leading white space is now treated as a field separator, so $1 is always the label and $2 is always the operator.

Because the "op code" for const is zero, the single assignment

```
mem[nextmem++] = 1000 * op[$1] + $2   # pack into word
```

can be used to store both constants and instructions in pass 2.

Exercise 6-1. Modify asm to print the listing of memory and program shown above. □

Exercise 6-2. Augment the interpreter to print a trace of the instructions as they are executed. □

Exercise 6-3. To get an idea of scale, add code to handle errors, deal with a richer set of conditional jumps, etc. How would you handle literal operands like add =1 instead of forcing the user to create a cell called one? □

Exercise 6-4. Write a disassembler that converts a raw memory dump into assembly language. □

Exercise 6-5. Look at a real machine (e.g., the 6502, as found in Apple-II and Commodore, or the 8086 family in the IBM PC and compatibles) and try writing an assembler for a subset of its instructions. □

6.2   A Language for Drawing Graphs

The lexical and syntactic simplicity of our assembly language made its analysis easy to do with field splitting. This same simplicity also appears in some higher-level languages. Our next example is a processor for a prototype language called graph, for plotting graphs of data. The input is a graph specification in which each line is a data point or labeling information for the coordinate axes. Data points are x-y pairs, or y values for which a default sequence of x values 1, 2, 3, etc., is to be generated. An optional nonnumeric plotting character can follow either form of data value. Labeling information consists of a keyword and parameter values:

```
label caption
range xmin ymin xmax ymax
left ticks t₁ t₂ ...
bottom ticks t₁ t₂ ...
height number
width number
```

These lines can appear in any order. They are all optional; in particular, there is no need to specify the range of data values.

The processor scales the data points and produces commands to plot them in a suitable form. To make the discussion concrete, we will simply print them out as a 24×80 character array, but it would be easy to produce plotting commands for some graphics device instead. For example, this input:

```
label Annual Traffic Deaths, USA, 1925-1984
range 1920 5000 1990 60000
left ticks 10000 30000 50000
bottom ticks 1930 1940 1950 1960 1970 1980

1925 21800
1930 31050
1935 36369
...
1981 51500
1982 46000
1983 44600
1984 46200
```

produces this output:

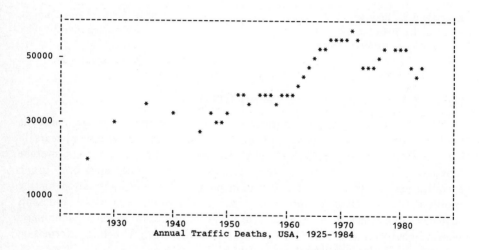

Annual Traffic Deaths, USA, 1925-1984

The graph processor operates in two phases. The main loop reads the graph specification and parses it, using patterns to recognize the different types of statements. The intermediate representation of the graph is stored in various arrays and variables. From this representation, the END action computes the range of values if necessary, then draws a frame, the ticks, the label, and the data points. The output operations have been written as separate functions to localize changes for specific devices.

This is by far the largest awk program we have seen so far; at one hundred lines, it's the second largest in the book. In spite of that, the individual pieces are quite short and simple. It was written in small steps as well, as the design evolved.

```
# graph - processor for a graph-drawing language
#    input:  data and specification of a graph
#    output: data plotted in specified area

BEGIN {                      # set frame dimensions...
    ht = 24; wid = 80  # height and width
    ox = 6; oy = 2       # offset for x and y axes
    number = "^[-+]?([0-9]+[.]?[0-9]*¦[.][0-9]+)" \
                            "([eE][-+]?[0-9]+)?$"
}
$1 == "label" {                            # for bottom
    sub(/^ *label */, "")
    botlab = $0
    next
}
$1 == "bottom" && $2 == "ticks" {      # ticks for x-axis
    for (i = 3; i <= NF; i++) bticks[++nb] = $i
    next
}
$1 == "left" && $2 == "ticks" {        # ticks for y-axis
    for (i = 3; i <= NF; i++) lticks[++nl] = $i
    next
}
$1 == "range" {                         # xmin ymin xmax ymax
    xmin = $2; ymin = $3; xmax = $4; ymax = $5
    next
}
$1 == "height" { ht = $2; next }
$1 == "width"  { wid = $2; next }
$1 ~ number && $2 ~ number {          # pair of numbers
    nd++     # count number of data points
    x[nd] = $1; y[nd] = $2
    ch[nd] = $3    # optional plotting character
    next
}
$1 ~ number && $2 !~ number {          # single number
    nd++     # count number of data points
    x[nd] = nd; y[nd] = $1; ch[nd] = $2
    next
}
END {     # draw graph
    if (xmin == "") {           # no range was given
        xmin = xmax = x[1]       # so compute it
        ymin = ymax = y[1]
        for (i = 2; i <= nd; i++) {
            if (x[i] < xmin) xmin = x[i]
            if (x[i] > xmax) xmax = x[i]
            if (y[i] < ymin) ymin = y[i]
            if (y[i] > ymax) ymax = y[i]
        }
    }
    frame(); ticks(); label(); data(); draw()
}
```

```
function frame() {          # create frame for graph
    for (i = ox; i < wid; i++) plot(i, oy, "-")        # bottom
    for (i = ox; i < wid; i++) plot(i, ht-1, "-")      # top
    for (i = oy; i < ht; i++) plot(ox, i, "¦")         # left
    for (i = oy; i < ht; i++) plot(wid-1, i, "¦")      # right
}
function ticks(    i) {    # create tick marks for both axes
    for (i = 1; i <= nb; i++) {
        plot(xscale(bticks[i]), oy, "¦")
        splot(xscale(bticks[i])-1, 1, bticks[i])
    }
    for (i = 1; i <= nl; i++) {
        plot(ox, yscale(lticks[i]), "-")
        splot(0, yscale(lticks[i]), lticks[i])
    }
}
function label() {          # center label under x-axis
    splot(int((wid + ox - length(botlab))/2), 0, botlab)
}
function data(    i) {      # create data points
    for (i = 1; i <= nd; i++)
        plot(xscale(x[i]),yscale(y[i]),ch[i]=="" ? "*" : ch[i])
}
function draw(    i, j) { # print graph from array
    for (i = ht-1; i >= 0; i--) {
        for (j = 0; j < wid; j++)
            printf((j,i) in array ? array[j,i] : " ")
        printf("\n")
    }
}
function xscale(x) {        # scale x-value
    return int((x-xmin)/(xmax-xmin) * (wid-1-ox) + ox + 0.5)
}
function yscale(y) {        # scale y-value
    return int((y-ymin)/(ymax-ymin) * (ht-1-oy) + oy + 0.5)
}
function plot(x, y, c) {  # put character c in array
    array[x,y] = c
}
function splot(x, y, s,    i, n) { # put string s in array
    n = length(s)
    for (i = 0; i < n; i++)
        array[x+i, y] = substr(s, i+1, 1)
}
```

The graph language falls naturally into the pattern-directed model of computation that awk itself supports: the specification statements are keywords with values. This style is often a good start for any language design; it seems easy for people to use, and it is certainly easy to process.

Our language graph is a simplified version of the graph-plotting language grap, which is a preprocessor for the pic picture-drawing language. The same

data and a description almost identical to that above produces this picture when
run through `grap`, `pic` and `troff`:

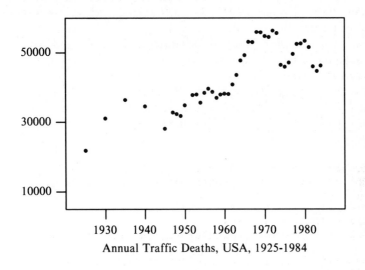

Annual Traffic Deaths, USA, 1925-1984

Awk is good for designing and experimenting with little languages. If a
design proves suitable, a production version can be recoded in a more efficient
systems language like C. In some cases, the prototype version itself may be
suitable for production use. These situations typically involve sugar-coating or
specializing an existing tool.

A specific instance is the preparation of specialized graphs, where we have
used awk programs to translate simple languages into `grap` commands. Examples include scatter-plot matrices, dotcharts (a form of histogram), boxplots
(which show mean, quartiles and extremes of a set of observations), and pie-
charts.

Exercise 6-6. Modify `graph` so that the graph can be drawn transposed, that is, with
the *x* axis running down the page and the *y* axis across the page. Also add the ability to
specify logarithmic *x* and *y* scales. □

Exercise 6-7. Add a command to `graph` that can be used to cause data to be read from
a file. □

Exercise 6-8. Compute suitable tick locations automatically. (Awk is good for experimenting with algorithms for this task even if the final implementation will be in another
language.) □

Exercise 6-9. If your system provides some plotting library, extend or modify `graph` to
generate commands for it. (This is an example of sugar-coating.) □

6.3   A Sort Generator

The Unix sort command is versatile *if* you know how to use it. But it's hard to remember all the options, and numbering fields from zero may be counter to your intuition. So as another exercise in little-language design, we will develop a language `sortgen` to generate sort commands from a more English-like specification. The `sortgen` processor generates a sort command but does not run it — that task is left to the user, who may want to review the command before invoking it.

The input to `sortgen` is a sequence of words and phrases describing sort options like the field separator, the sort keys, and the nature and direction of comparisons. The goal is to cover the common cases with a forgiving syntax. For example, given this input:

```
descending numeric order
```

the output is

```
sort -rn
```

As a more complicated example, with this description:

```
field separator is :
primary key is field 1
    increasing alphabetic
secondary key is field 5
    reverse numeric
```

`sortgen` produces a sort command equivalent to the first one in Chapter 4:

```
sort -t':' +0 -1 +4rn -5
```

The heart of `sortgen` is a set of rules to translate words and phrases describing sort options into corresponding flags for the sort command. The rules are implemented by pattern-action statements in which the patterns are regular expressions that match the phrases describing sort options; the actions compute the appropriate flags for the sort command. For instance, any mention of "unique" or "discard identical" is taken as a request for the -u option, which discards duplicate items. Similarly, the field separator character is assumed to be either a tab or a single character that appears somewhere on a line containing some form of the word "separate."

The hardest part is dealing with multiple sort keys, each of which can span multiple fields. Here the magic word is "key," which has to appear in the input. When it does, one or two isolated numbers are collected as the field numbers. Each mention of "key" starts collection of options for a new key. Per-key options include blank suppression (-b), dictionary order (-d), folding of upper and lower case together (-f), numeric order (-n), and reversal (-r).

```
# sortgen - generate sort command
#    input:   sequence of lines describing sorting options
#    output: Unix sort command with appropriate arguments

BEGIN { key = 0 }

/no ¦not ¦n't / { print "error: can't do negatives:", $0; ok = 1 }

# rules for global options
        { ok = 0 }
/uniq¦discard.*(iden¦dupl)/   { uniq = " -u"; ok = 1 }
/separ.*tab¦tab.*sep/         { sep = "t'\t'"; ok = 1 }
/separ/ { for (i = 1; i <= NF; i++)
                if (length($i) == 1)
                    sep = "t'" $i "'"
          ok = 1
        }
/key/   { key++; dokey(); ok = 1 } # new key; must come in order

# rules for each key

/dict/                        { dict[key] = "d"; ok = 1 }
/ignore.*(space¦blank)/       { blank[key] = "b"; ok = 1 }
/fold¦case/                   { fold[key] = "f"; ok = 1 }
/num/                         { num[key] = "n"; ok = 1 }
/rev¦descend¦decreas¦down¦oppos/  { rev[key] = "r"; ok = 1 }
/forward¦ascend¦increas¦up¦alpha/ { next }    # this is sort's default
!ok    { print "error: can't understand:", $0 }

END {                         # print flags for each key
    cmd = "sort" uniq
    flag = dict[0] blank[0] fold[0] rev[0] num[0] sep
    if (flag) cmd = cmd " -" flag
    for (i = 1; i <= key; i++)
        if (pos[i] != "") {
                flag = pos[i] dict[i] blank[i] fold[i] rev[i] num[i]
                if (flag) cmd = cmd " +" flag
                if (pos2[i]) cmd = cmd " -" pos2[i]
        }
    print cmd
}

function dokey(   i) {        # determine position of key
    for (i = 1; i <= NF; i++)
        if ($i ~ /^[0-9]+$/) {
                pos[key] = $i - 1    # sort uses 0-origin
                break
        }
    for (i++; i <= NF; i++)
        if ($i ~ /^[0-9]+$/) {
                pos2[key] = $i
                break
        }
    if (pos[key] == "")
        printf("error: invalid key specification: %s\n", $0)
    if (pos2[key] == "")
        pos2[key] = pos[key] + 1
}
```

To avoid dealing with input like "don't discard duplicates" or "no numeric data," the first pattern of `sortgen` rejects lines that appear to be phrased negatively. Subsequent rules deal with the global options, then with those that apply only to the current key. The program informs the user of any line it was unable to understand.

This program is still easy to fool, of course, but if one is trying to get the right answer, not to provoke an error, `sortgen` is already useful.

Exercise 6-10. Write a version of `sortgen` that provides access to all the facilities of the sort command on your system. Detect inconsistent requests, such as sorting numerically and in dictionary order simultaneously. □

Exercise 6-11. How much more accurate can you make `sortgen` without making its input language significantly more formal? □

Exercise 6-12. Write a program that translates a sort command into an English sentence. Run `sortgen` on its output. □

6.4   A Reverse-Polish Calculator

Suppose we want a calculator program for balancing a checkbook or evaluating arithmetic expressions. Awk itself is perfectly reasonable for such calculations except that we have to re-run it each time the program changes. We need a program that will read and evaluate expressions as they are typed.

To avoid writing a parser, we will require the user to write expressions in reverse-Polish notation. (It's called "reverse" because operators follow their operands, and "Polish" after the Polish mathematician Jan Lukasiewicz, who first proposed the notation.) The normal "infix" expression

```
(1 + 2) * (3 - 4) / 5
```

is written in reverse Polish as

```
1 2 + 3 4 - * 5 /
```

No parentheses are needed — expressions are unambiguous if the number of operands taken by each operator is known. Reverse-Polish expressions are easy to parse and evaluate using a stack and, as a consequence, programming languages like Forth and Postscript, and some pocket calculators, use this notation.

Our first calculator provides nothing more than the ability to evaluate arithmetic expressions written in reverse-Polish notation, with all operators and operands separated by blanks. If a field is a number, it is pushed onto a stack; if it is an operator, the proper operation is done to the operands on the top of the stack. The value at the top of the stack is printed and popped at the end of each input line.

```
# calc1 - reverse-Polish calculator, version 1
#   input:  arithmetic expressions in reverse Polish
#   output: values of expressions

{   for (i = 1; i <= NF; i++)
        if ($i ~ /^[+-]?([0-9]+[.]?[0-9]*|[.][0-9]+)$/) {
            stack[++top] = $i
        } else if ($i == "+" && top > 1) {
            stack[top-1] += stack[top]; top--
        } else if ($i == "-" && top > 1) {
            stack[top-1] -= stack[top]; top--
        } else if ($i == "*" && top > 1) {
            stack[top-1] *= stack[top]; top--
        } else if ($i == "/" && top > 1) {
            stack[top-1] /= stack[top]; top--
        } else if ($i == "^" && top > 1) {
            stack[top-1] ^= stack[top]; top--
        } else {
            printf("error: cannot evaluate %s\n", $i)
            top = 0
            next
        }
    if (top == 1)
        printf("\t%.8g\n", stack[top--])
    else if (top > 1) {
        printf("error: too many operands\n")
        top = 0
    }
}
```

For the input

```
1 2 + 3 4 - * 5 /
```

calc1 gives the answer -0.6.

Our second reverse-Polish calculator provides user-defined variables and access to a handful of arithmetic functions. Variable names consist of a letter followed by letters or digits; the special syntax *var=* pops the value on the top of the stack and assigns it to the variable *var*. If the input line ends with an assignment, no value is printed. Thus a typical interaction might look like this (program output is indented):

```
0 -1 atan2 pi=
pi
      3.1415927
355 113 / x= x
      3.1415929
x pi /
      1.0000001
2 sqrt
      1.4142136
```

The program is a straightforward extension of the previous one:

```
# calc2 - reverse-Polish calculator, version 2
#     input:  expressions in reverse Polish
#     output: value of each expression

{ for (i = 1; i <= NF; i++)
      if ($i ~ /^[+-]?([0-9]+[.]?[0-9]*¦[.][0-9]+)$/) {
          stack[++top] = $i
      } else if ($i == "+" && top > 1) {
          stack[top-1] += stack[top]; top--
      } else if ($i == "-" && top > 1) {
          stack[top-1] -= stack[top]; top--
      } else if ($i == "*" && top > 1) {
          stack[top-1] *= stack[top]; top--
      } else if ($i == "/" && top > 1) {
          stack[top-1] /= stack[top]; top--
      } else if ($i == "^" && top > 1) {
          stack[top-1] ^= stack[top]; top--
      } else if ($i == "sin" && top > 0) {
          stack[top] = sin(stack[top])
      } else if ($i == "cos" && top > 0) {
          stack[top] = cos(stack[top])
      } else if ($i == "atan2" && top > 1) {
          stack[top-1] = atan2(stack[top-1],stack[top]); top--
      } else if ($i == "log" && top > 0) {
          stack[top] = log(stack[top])
      } else if ($i == "exp" && top > 0) {
          stack[top] = exp(stack[top])
      } else if ($i == "sqrt" && top > 0) {
          stack[top] = sqrt(stack[top])
      } else if ($i == "int" && top > 0) {
          stack[top] = int(stack[top])
      } else if ($i in vars) {
          stack[++top] = vars[$i]
      } else if ($i ~ /^[a-zA-Z][a-zA-Z0-9]*=$/ && top > 0) {
          vars[substr($i, 1, length($i)-1)] = stack[top--]
      } else {
          printf("error: cannot evaluate %s\n", $i)
          top = 0
          next
      }
  if (top == 1 && $NF !~ /\=$/)
      printf("\t%.8g\n", stack[top--])
  else if (top > 1) {
      printf("error: too many operands\n")
      top = 0
  }
}
```

Exercise 6-13. Add built-in variables for standard values like π and e to calc2. Add a built-in variable for the result of the last input line. Add stack-manipulation operators to duplicate the top of the stack and to swap the top two items. □

6.5   An Infix Calculator

So far, the languages we have considered in this chapter have all had a syntax that was easy to analyze. Most high-level languages, however, have operators at many different precedence levels, nested structures such as parentheses and if-then-else statements, and other constructions that require more powerful parsing techniques than field splitting or regular expression pattern matching. It is possible to process such languages in awk by writing a full-fledged parser, as one would in any language. In this section we will construct a program to evaluate arithmetic expressions in the familiar "infix" notation; this is a useful precursor to the much larger parser in the next section.

Arithmetic expressions with the operators +, -, *, and / can be described by a grammar in the same style as the one we used in Chapter 5:

$$
\begin{array}{lcl}
\textit{expr} & \rightarrow & \textit{term} \\
              &   & \textit{expr + term} \\
              &   & \textit{expr - term} \\
\textit{term} & \rightarrow & \textit{factor} \\
              &   & \textit{term * factor} \\
              &   & \textit{term / factor} \\
\textit{factor} & \rightarrow & \textit{number} \\
                &   & \textit{(expr)}
\end{array}
$$

This grammar captures not only the form of arithmetic expressions but also the precedences and associativities of the operators. For example, an *expr* is the sum or difference of *term*'s, but a *term* is made up of *factor*'s, which assures that multiplication and division are dealt with before addition or subtraction.

We can think of the process of parsing as one of diagramming a sentence, the opposite of the generation process discussed in Chapter 5. For example, the expression 1 + 2 * 3 is parsed like this:

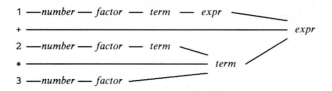

To make an infix evaluator, we need a parser for expressions. With a little effort, the grammar can be used to construct the parser and organize the program as well. A function is written to process each nonterminal in the grammar: the program uses the function `expr` to process *term*'s separated by plus or minus signs, the function `term` to process *factor*'s separated by multiplication or division signs, and the function `factor` to recognize numbers and process parenthesized *expr*'s.

In the following program, each input line is taken as a single expression, which is evaluated and printed. We are still requiring that all operators and operands, including parentheses, be separated by blanks. The variable f points to the next field to be examined, which is the next operator or operand.

```
# calc3 - infix calculator

NF > 0 {
    f = 1
    e = expr()
    if (f <= NF) printf("error at %s\n", $f)
    else printf("\t%.8g\n", e)
}

function expr(  e) {          # term ¦ term [+-] term
    e = term()
    while ($f == "+" ¦¦ $f == "-")
        e = $(f++) == "+" ? e + term() : e - term()
    return e
}

function term(  e) {          # factor ¦ factor [*/] factor
    e = factor()
    while ($f == "*" ¦¦ $f == "/")
        e = $(f++) == "*" ? e * factor() : e / factor()
    return e
}

function factor(  e) {        # number ¦ (expr)
    if ($f ~ /^[+-]?([0-9]+[.]?[0-9]*¦[.][0-9]+)$/) {
        return $(f++)
    } else if ($f == "(") {
        f++
        e = expr()
        if ($(f++) != ")")
            printf("error: missing ) at %s\n", $f)
        return e
    } else {
        printf("error: expected number or ( at %s\n", $f)
        return 0
    }
}
```

The construction $(f++) produces the value of $f, then increments f; it is not the same as $f++, which increments the value of $f.

Exercise 6-14. Construct a set of inputs to test calc3 thoroughly. □

Exercise 6-15. Add exponentiation, built-in functions, and variables to the infix calculator calc3. How does the implementation compare to the reverse-Polish version? □

Exercise 6-16. Improve the error-handling performance of calc3. □

6.6 Recursive-Descent Parsing

In this section, we develop a recursive-descent translator for a small subset of awk, written in awk itself. The part that deals with arithmetic expressions is essentially the same as in the previous section. To add some verisimilitude to the exercise, we have chosen to generate C code as the target program, with function calls replacing awk's operators. This is partly to illustrate the principles of syntax-directed translation, and partly to suggest a way to create a "C version" of awk that could run faster and be easier to extend. The general approach is to replace every arithmetic operator by a function call; for example, x=y becomes `assign(x,y)`, and x+y becomes `eval("+",x,y)`. The main input loop is expressed as a `while` that calls a function `getrec` to read each input line and split it into fields. Thus,

```
BEGIN    { x = 0; y = 1 }

$1 > x   { if (x == y+1) {
               x = 1
               y = x * 2
           } else
               print x, z[x]
         }

NR > 1   { print $1 }

END      { print NR }
```

is translated into this C code:

```
assign(x, num((float)0));
assign(y, num((float)1));
while (getrec()) {
    if (eval(">", field(num((float)1)), x)) {
        if (eval("==", x, eval("+", y, num((float)1)))) {
            assign(x, num((float)1));
            assign(y, eval("*", x, num((float)2)));
        } else {
            print(x, array(z, x));
        }
    }
    if (eval(">", NR, num((float)1))) {
        print(field(num((float)1)));
    }
}
print(NR);
```

A good way to approach the design of the front end of a language processor is to write down a grammar for the input language. Using the notation of Section 5.1, our subset of awk has this grammar:

program	→	*opt-begin pa-stats opt-end*
opt-begin	→	`BEGIN` *statlist* | `""`
opt-end	→	`END` *statlist* | `""`
pa-stats	→	*statlist* | *pattern* | *pattern statlist*
pattern	→	*expr*
statlist	→	`{` *stats* `}`
stats	→	*stat stats* | `""`
stat	→	`print` *exprlist* |
		`if (` *expr* `)` *stat opt-else* |
		`while (` *expr* `)` *stat* |
		statlist |
		ident `=` *expr*
opt-else	→	`else` *stat* | `""`
exprlist	→	*expr* | *expr* `,` *exprlist*
expr	→	*number* | *ident* | `$`*expr* | `(` *expr* `)* |
		expr `<` *expr* | *expr* `<=` *expr* | ... | *expr* `>` *expr* |
		expr `+` *expr* | *expr* `-` *expr* |
		expr `*` *expr* | *expr* `/` *expr* | *expr* `%` *expr*
ident	→	*name* | *name*`[`*expr*`]` | *name*`(`*exprlist*`)`

The notation `""` stands for the null string and | separates alternatives.

The key ingredient in a recursive-descent parser is a set of recursive parsing routines, each of which is responsible for identifying, in the input, strings generated by a nonterminal in the grammar. Each routine calls in turn upon others to help out in the task until the terminal level is reached, at which point actual tokens of input are read and categorized. The recursive, top-down nature of this method of parsing leads to the name "recursive descent."

The structure of the parsing routines closely matches the grammatical structure of the language. For example, the function for `program` looks for an optional `BEGIN` action, followed by a list of pattern-action statements, followed by an optional `END` action.

In our recursive-descent parser, lexical analysis is done by a routine called `advance`, which finds the next token and assigns it to the variable `tok`. Output is produced each time a *stat* is identified; lower-level routines return strings that are combined into larger units. An attempt has been made to keep the output readable by inserting tabs; the proper level of nesting is maintained in the variable `nt`.

The program is by no means complete — it does not parse all of awk, nor does it generate all of the C code that would be needed even for this subset — and it is not at all robust. But it does do enough to demonstrate how the whole thing might be done, and it also shows the structure of a recursive-descent translator for a nontrivial fraction of a real language.

```
# awk.parser - recursive-descent translator for part of awk
#    input:  awk program (very restricted subset)
#    output: C code to implement the awk program

BEGIN { program() }

function advance() {       # lexical analyzer; returns next token
    if (tok == "(eof)") return "(eof)"
    while (length(line) == 0)
        if (getline line == 0)
            return tok = "(eof)"
    sub(/^[ \t]+/, "", line)   # remove white space
    if (match(line, /^[A-Za-z_][A-Za-z_0-9]*/) ||     # identifier
        match(line, /^-?([0-9]+\.?[0-9]*|\.[0-9]+)/) ||  # number
        match(line, /^(<|<=|==|!=|>=|>)/) ||          # relational
        match(line, /^./)) {                    # everything else
            tok = substr(line, 1, RLENGTH)
            line = substr(line, RLENGTH+1)
            return tok
        }
    error("line " NR " incomprehensible at " line)
}
function gen(s) {      # print s with nt leading tabs
    printf("%s%s\n", substr("\t\t\t\t\t\t\t\t\t", 1, nt), s)
}
function eat(s) {      # read next token if s == tok
    if (tok != s) error("line " NR ": saw " tok ", expected " s)
    advance()
}
function nl() {        # absorb newlines and semicolons
    while (tok == "\n" || tok == ";")
        advance()
}
function error(s) { print "Error: " s | "cat 1>&2"; exit 1 }

function program() {
    advance()
    if (tok == "BEGIN") { eat("BEGIN"); statlist() }
    pastats()
    if (tok == "END") { eat("END"); statlist() }
    if (tok != "(eof)") error("program continues after END")
}
function pastats() {
    gen("while (getrec()) {"); nt++
    while (tok != "END" && tok != "(eof)") pastat()
    nt--; gen("}")
}
function pastat() {   # pattern-action statement
    if (tok == "{")         # action only
        statlist()
    else {                  # pattern-action
        gen("if (" pattern() ") {"); nt++
        if (tok == "{") statlist()
        else            # default action is print $0
            gen("print(field(0));")
        nt--; gen("}")
    }
}
```

```
function pattern() { return expr() }

function statlist() {
    eat("{"); nl(); while (tok != "}") stat(); eat("}"); nl()
}

function stat() {
    if (tok == "print") { eat("print"); gen("print(" exprlist() ");") }
    else if (tok == "if") ifstat()
    else if (tok == "while") whilestat()
    else if (tok == "{") statlist()
    else gen(simplestat() ";")
    nl()
}

function ifstat() {
    eat("if"); eat("("); gen("if (" expr() ") {"); eat(")"); nl(); nt++
    stat()
    if (tok == "else") {         # optional else
        eat("else")
        nl(); nt--; gen("} else {"); nt++
        stat()
    }
    nt--; gen("}")
}

function whilestat() {
    eat("while"); eat("("); gen("while (" expr() ") {"); eat(")"); nl()
    nt++; stat(); nt--; gen("}")
}

function simplestat(   lhs) { # ident = expr ¦ name(exprlist)
    lhs = ident()
    if (tok == "=") {
        eat("=")
        return "assign(" lhs ", " expr() ")"
    } else return lhs
}

function exprlist(    n, e) { # expr , expr , ...
    e = expr()          # has to be at least one
    for (n = 1; tok == ","; n++) {
        advance()
        e = e ", " expr()
    }
    return e
}

function expr(e) {                 # rel ¦ rel relop rel
    e = rel()
    while (tok ~ /<¦<=¦==¦¦!=¦>=¦>/) {
        op = tok
        advance()
        e = sprintf("eval(\"%s\", %s, %s)", op, e, rel())
    }
    return e
}
```

```
function rel(op, e) {            # term | term [+-] term
    e = term()
    while (tok == "+" || tok == "-") {
        op = tok
        advance()
        e = sprintf("eval(\"%s\", %s, %s)", op, e, term())
    }
    return e
}

function term(op, e) {           # fact | fact [*/%] fact
    e = fact()
    while (tok == "*" || tok == "/" || tok == "%") {
        op = tok
        advance()
        e = sprintf("eval(\"%s\", %s, %s)", op, e, fact())
    }
    return e
}

function fact(  e) {             # (expr) | $fact | ident | number
    if (tok == "(") {
        eat("("); e = expr(); eat(")")
        return "(" e ")"
    } else if (tok == "$") {
        eat("$")
        return "field(" fact() ")"
    } else if (tok ~ /^[A-Za-z][A-Za-z0-9]*/) {
        return ident()
    } else if (tok ~ /^-?([0-9]+\.?[0-9]*|\.[0-9]+)/) {
        e = tok
        advance()
        return "num((float)" e ")"
    } else
        error("unexpected " tok " at line " NR)
}

function ident(  id, e) {        # name | name[expr] | name(exprlist)
    if (!match(tok, /^[A-Za-z_][A-Za-z_0-9]*/))
        error("unexpected " tok " at line " NR)
    id = tok
    advance()
    if (tok == "[") {            # array
        eat("["); e = expr(); eat("]")
        return "array(" id ", " e ")"
    } else if (tok == "(") {  # function call
        eat("(")
        if (tok != ")") {
            e = exprlist()
            eat(")")
        } else eat(")")
        return id "(" e ")"      # calls are statements
    } else
        return id                # variable
}
```

6.7 Summary

Building a little language is often a productive approach to a programming task. Awk is convenient for translating languages in which lexical analysis and parsing can be done with field splitting and regular expression pattern matching. Associative arrays are good for storing symbol-table information. The pattern-action structure matches pattern-directed languages.

The design choices for new languages in new application areas are often difficult to make without some experimentation. In awk it is easy to construct prototypes for feasibility experiments. The results may suggest modifications to an initial design before a large investment in implementation has been made. Once a successful prototype processor has been created, it is relatively straightforward to transcribe the prototype into a production model using compiler-construction tools like `lex` and `yacc`, and compiled programming languages like C.

Bibliographic Notes

The assembler and interpreter are patterned after one developed by Jon Bentley and John Dallen for a software engineering course; their experience is described in "Exercises in software design," *IEEE Transactions on Software Engineering*, 1987.

The `grap` language for typesetting graphs is described in an article by Jon Bentley and Brian Kernighan in *Communications of the ACM*, August, 1986. That issue also contains a *Programming Pearls* column by Bentley on "Little Languages."

For more discussion of how to construct a recursive-descent translator from a grammar, see Chapter 2 of *Compilers: Principles, Techniques, and Tools*, by Aho, Sethi, and Ullman (Addison-Wesley, 1986).

7   EXPERIMENTS WITH ALGORITHMS

Often the best way to understand how something works is to build it and do some experiments. This is particularly true for algorithms: writing code illuminates and clarifies issues that are too easily glossed over with pseudo-code. Furthermore, the resulting programs can be tested to ensure that they behave as advertised, which is not true of pseudo-code.

Awk is a good tool for this kind of experimentation. If a program is written in awk, it's easy to concentrate on the algorithm instead of language details. If the algorithm is ultimately to be part of a larger program, it may be more productive to get it working in isolation first. Small awk programs are also excellent for building a scaffold for debugging, testing, and performance evaluation, regardless of what language the algorithm itself was implemented in.

This chapter illustrates experiments with algorithms. The first half describes three sorting methods that are usually encountered in a first course on algorithms, with awk programs for testing, performance measurement, and profiling. The second half shows several topological sorting algorithms that culminate in a version of the Unix file-updating utility make.

7.1   Sorting

This section covers three well-known and useful algorithms: insertion sort, quicksort, and heapsort. Insertion sort is short and simple, but efficient only for sorting a few elements; quicksort is one of the best general-purpose sorting techniques; heapsort optimizes worst-case performance. For each of these algorithms, we will give the basic ideas, show an implementation, present testing routines, and evaluate the performance.

Insertion Sort

Basic idea. Insertion sort is similar to the method of sorting a sequence of cards by picking up the cards one at a time and inserting each card into its proper position in the hand.

Implementation. The following code uses this method to sort an array
A[1], ..., A[n] into increasing order. The first action reads the input a line at
a time into the array; the END action calls isort, then prints the results:

```
# insertion sort

    { A[NR] = $0 }

END { isort(A, NR)
      for (i = 1; i <= NR; i++)
          print A[i]
    }

# isort - sort A[1..n] by insertion

function isort(A,n,    i,j,t) {
    for (i = 2; i <= n; i++)
        for (j = i; j > 1 && A[j-1] > A[j]; j--) {
            # swap A[j-1] and A[j]
            t = A[j-1]; A[j-1] = A[j]; A[j] = t
        }
}
```

Elements 1 through $i-1$ of A are in order at the beginning of the outer loop of
isort. The inner loop moves the element currently in the i-th position towards
the beginning of the array past any larger elements. At the end of the outer
loop, all *n* elements will be in order.

This program will sort numbers or strings equally well. But beware of mixed
input — the comparisons will sometimes be surprising because of coercions.

If at the beginning A contains the eight integers

```
8 1 6 3 5 2 4 7
```

the array passes through the following configurations:

```
8¦1 6 3 5 2 4 7
1 8¦6 3 5 2 4 7
1 6 8¦3 5 2 4 7
1 3 6 8¦5 2 4 7
1 3 5 6 8¦2 4 7
1 2 3 5 6 8¦4 7
1 2 3 4 5 6 8¦7
1 2 3 4 5 6 7 8¦
```

The vertical bar separates the sorted part of the array from the elements that
have yet to be considered.

Testing. How should we test isort? We could just type at it to see what
happens. That's a necessary first step, of course, but for a program of any size
it's not a substitute for more careful testing. A second possibility is to generate
a large number of sets of random numbers and check the outputs. That's certainly an improvement, but we can do even better with a small set of tests by a

systematic attack on places where code usually goes wrong — the boundaries
and special cases. For sorting routines, those might include the following:

> a sequence of length 0 (the empty input)
> a sequence of length 1 (a single number)
> a sequence of *n* random numbers
> a sequence of *n* sorted numbers
> a sequence of *n* numbers sorted in reverse order
> a sequence of *n* identical numbers

One of the goals of this chapter is to show how awk can be used to help with
testing and evaluation of programs. Let us illustrate by mechanizing test generation and evaluation of results for the sorting routines.

There are two distinct approaches, each with its advantages. The first might
be called "batch mode": write a program to execute a pre-planned set of tests,
exercising the sort function as suggested above. The following routines generate
the data and check the results. In addition to isort itself, there are functions
for creating arrays of various types of data and for checking whether the array
is sorted.

```
# batch test of sorting routines

BEGIN {
    print "     0 elements"
    isort(A, 0); check(A, 0)
    print "     1 element"
    genid(A, 1); isort(A, 1); check(A, 1)

    n = 10
    print "    " n " random integers"
    genrand(A, n); isort(A, n); check(A, n)

    print "    " n " sorted integers"
    gensort(A, n); isort(A, n); check(A, n)

    print "    " n " reverse-sorted integers"
    genrev(A, n); isort(A, n); check(A, n)

    print "    " n " identical integers"
    genid(A, n); isort(A, n); check(A, n)
}


function isort(A,n,     i,j,t) {
    for (i = 2; i <= n; i++)
        for (j = i; j > 1 && A[j-1] > A[j]; j--) {
            # swap A[j-1] and A[j]
            t = A[j-1]; A[j-1] = A[j]; A[j] = t
        }
}
```

```
# test-generation and sorting routines...

function check(A,n,   i) {
    for (i = 1; i < n; i++)
        if (A[i] > A[i+1])
            printf("array is not sorted, element %d\n", i)
}

function genrand(A,n,  i) { # put n random integers in A
    for (i = 1; i <= n; i++)
        A[i] = int(n*rand())
}

function gensort(A,n,  i) { # put n sorted integers in A
    for (i = 1; i <= n; i++)
        A[i] = i
}

function genrev(A,n,  i) {  # put n reverse-sorted integers
    for (i = 1; i <= n; i++)  # in A
        A[i] = n+1-i
}

function genid(A,n,  i) {   # put n identical integers in A
    for (i = 1; i <= n; i++)
        A[i] = 1
}
```

The second approach to testing is somewhat less conventional, but particularly suited to awk. The idea is to build a framework that makes it easy to do tests interactively. This style is a nice complement to batch testing, especially when the algorithm in question is less well understood than sorting. It's also convenient when the task is debugging.

Specifically, we will design what is in effect a tiny language for creating test data and operations. Since the language doesn't have to do much or deal with a big user population, it doesn't have to be very complicated. It's also easy to throw the code away and start over if necessary. Our language provides for automatic generation of an array of n elements of some type, for explicit specification of the data array, and, looking ahead to the rest of this chapter, for naming the sort to be exercised. We have omitted the sorting and data generation routines, which are the same as in the previous example.

The basic organization of the program is just a sequence of regular expressions that scan the input to determine the type of data and type of sorting algorithm to use. If the input doesn't match any of these patterns, an error message suggests how to use it correctly. This is often more useful than merely saying that the input was wrong.

```
# interactive test framework for sort routines

/^[0-9]+.*rand/ { n = $1; genrand(A, n); dump(A, n); next }
/^[0-9]+.*id/   { n = $1; genid(A, n); dump(A, n); next }
/^[0-9]+.*sort/ { n = $1; gensort(A, n); dump(A, n); next }
/^[0-9]+.*rev/  { n = $1; genrev(A, n); dump(A, n); next }
/^data/ {    # use data right from this line
    for (i = 2; i <= NF; i++)
        A[i-1] = $i
    n = NF - 1
    next
}
/q.*sort/ { qsort(A, 1, n); check(A, n); dump(A, n); next }
/h.*sort/ { hsort(A, n); check(A, n); dump(A, n); next }
/i.*sort/ { isort(A, n); check(A, n); dump(A, n); next }
/./ { print "data ... ¦ N [rand¦id¦sort¦rev]; [qhi]sort" }

function dump(A, n) {    # print A[1]..A[n]
    for (i = 1; i <= n; i++)
        printf(" %s", A[i])
    printf("\n")
}

# test-generation and sorting routines ...
...
```

Regular expressions provide a forgiving input syntax; any phrase that looks remotely like "quicksort," for example, will result in a quicksort. We can also enter data directly as an alternative to automatic generation; this permits us to test the algorithms on text as well as numbers. To illustrate, here is a short dialog with the code above:

```
10 random
 9 8 4 6 7 2 4 0 4 0
isort
 0 0 2 4 4 4 6 7 8 9
10 reverse
 10 9 8 7 6 5 4 3 2 1
qsort
 1 2 3 4 5 6 7 8 9 10
data now is the time for all good men
hsort
 all for good is men now the time
```

Performance. The number of operations that `isort` performs depends on *n*, the number of items to be sorted, and on how sorted they already are. Insertion sort is a *quadratic* algorithm; that is, in the worst case, its running time grows as the square of the number of items being sorted. That means that sorting twice as many elements will take about four times as long. If the items happen to be almost in order already, however, there's much less work to do, so the running time grows linearly, that is, proportionally to the number of items.

The graph below shows how `isort` performs as a function of the number of elements to be sorted on three kinds of inputs: reverse-sorted, random, and equal-element sequences. We are counting comparisons and exchanges of items, which is a fair measure of the amount of work in a sorting procedure. As you can see, the performance of `isort` is worse for reverse-sorted sequences than it is for random sequences and both of these are much worse than equal-element sequences. The performance on a sorted sequence (not shown here) is similar to that for an equal-element sequence.

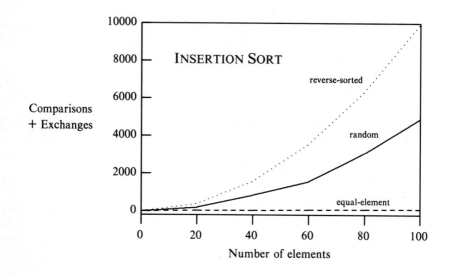

In summary, insertion sort is good for sorting small numbers of items, but its performance degrades badly as the number of items goes up, except when the input is almost sorted.

We generated the data for this graph and the others in this chapter by adding two counters to each sorting function, one for comparisons and one for exchanges. Here is the version of `isort` with counters:

```
function isort(A,n,      i,j,t) {  # insertion sort
    for (i = 2; i <= n; i++)        # with counters
        for (j = i; j > 1 && ++comp &&
            A[j-1] > A[j] && ++exch; j--) {
            # swap A[j-1] and A[j]
            t = A[j-1]; A[j-1] = A[j]; A[j] = t
        }
}
```

The counting is all done in one place, in the test of the inner `for` loop. Tests joined by `&&` are evaluated left to right until a term is false. The expression `++comp` is always true (pre-incrementing is mandatory here), so `comp` is

incremented precisely once per comparison of array elements, just before the
comparison. Then `exch` is incremented if and only if a pair is out of order.

The following program was used to organize the tests and prepare data for
plotting; again, it amounts to a tiny language that specifies parameters.

```
# test framework for sort performance evaluation
#    input:  lines with sort name, type of data, sizes...
#    output: name, type, size, comparisons, exchanges, c+e

{    for (i = 3; i <= NF; i++)
        test($1, $2, $i)
}

function test(sort, data, n) {
    comp = exch = 0
    if (data ~ /rand/)
        genrand(A, n)
    else if (data ~ /id/)
        genid(A, n)
    else if (data ~ /rev/)
        genrev(A, n)
    else
        print "illegal type of data in", $0
    if (sort ~ /q.*sort/)
        qsort(A, 1, n)
    else if (sort ~ /h.*sort/)
        hsort(A, n)
    else if (sort ~ /i.*sort/)
        isort(A, n)
    else print
        "illegal type of sort in", $0
    print sort, data, n, comp, exch, comp+exch
}

# test-generation and sorting routines ...
```

The input is a sequence of lines like

```
isort random 0 20 40 60 80 100
isort ident 0 20 40 60 80 100
```

and the output consists of lines containing the name, type, size, and counts for
each size. The output is fed into the graph-drawing program `grap`, a primitive
version of which was described in Chapter 6.

Exercise 7-1. The function `check` is actually not a very strong test. What kinds of
errors does it fail to detect? How would you implement more careful checking? □

Exercise 7-2. Most of our tests are based on sorting integers. How does `isort` perform
on other kinds of input? How would you modify the testing framework to handle more
general data? □

Exercise 7-3. We have tacitly assumed that each primitive operation takes constant
time. That is, accessing an array element, comparing two values, addition, assignment,

and so forth, each take a fixed amount of time. Is this a reasonable assumption for awk programs? Test it by writing programs that process large numbers of items. □

Quicksort

Basic idea. One of the most effective general-purpose sorting algorithms is a divide-and-conquer technique called quicksort, devised by C. A. R. Hoare in the early 1960's. To sort a sequence of elements, quicksort partitions the sequence into two subsequences and recursively sorts each of them. In the partition step, quicksort selects an element from the sequence as the partition element and divides the remaining elements into two groups: those less than the partition element, and those greater than or equal to it. These two groups are sorted by recursive calls to quicksort. If a sequence contains fewer than two elements, it is already sorted, so quicksort does nothing to it.

Implementation. There are several ways to implement quicksort, depending on how the partition step is done. Our method is simple to understand, though not necessarily the fastest. Since the algorithm is used recursively, we'll describe the partition step as it acts on a subarray `A[left]`, `A[left+1]`, ..., `A[right]`.

First, to choose the partition element, pick a random number `r` in the range `[left,right]`; any element could be chosen, but randomization works better when the data already has some order. The element `p` at position `r` in the array becomes the partition element. Then swap `A[left]` with `A[r]`. During the partition step the array holds the element `p` in `A[left]`, followed by the elements less than `p`, followed by the elements greater than or equal to `p`, followed by the as-yet unprocessed elements:

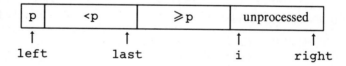

The index `last` points to the last element found to be less than `p` and the index `i` points to the next unprocessed element. Initially, `last` is equal to `left` and `i` is equal to `left+1`.

In the partition loop, we compare the element `A[i]` with `p`. If `A[i]` ⩾ `p`, we just increment `i`; if `A[i]` < `p`, we increment `last`, swap `A[last]` with `A[i]` and then increment `i`. Once we have processed all elements in the array in this manner, we swap `A[left]` with `A[last]`. At this point we have completed the partition step and the array looks like this:

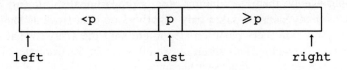

Now we apply the same process to the left and the right subarrays.

Suppose we use quicksort to sort an array with the eight elements

    8 1 6 3 5 2 4 7

At the first step we might select 4 as the partition element. The partition step would then rearrange the array around this element like this:

    2 1 3¦4¦5 6 8 7

We would then sort each of the subarrays 213 and 5687 recursively. The recursion ceases when a subarray has less than two elements.

The function qsort that implements quicksort is shown below. This program can be tested using the same testing routines that we gave for insertion sort.

```
# quicksort

    { A[NR] = $0 }

END { qsort(A, 1, NR)
      for (i = 1; i <= NR; i++)
          print A[i]
    }

# qsort - sort A[left..right] by quicksort

function qsort(A,left,right,    i,last) {
      if (left >= right)  # do nothing if array contains
          return          # less than two elements
      swap(A, left, left + int((right-left+1)*rand()))
      last = left   # A[left] is now partition element
      for (i = left+1; i <= right; i++)
          if (A[i] < A[left])
              swap(A, ++last, i)
      swap(A, left, last)
      qsort(A, left, last-1)
      qsort(A, last+1, right)
}

function swap(A,i,j,    t) {
      t = A[i]; A[i] = A[j]; A[j] = t
}
```

Performance. The number of operations that qsort performs depends on how evenly the partition element divides the array at each step. If the array is always split evenly, then the running time is proportional to $n\log n$. Thus sorting twice as many elements takes only slightly more than twice as long.

In the worst case every partition step might split the array so that one of the two subarrays is empty. This situation would occur if, for example, all elements were equal. In that case, quicksort becomes quadratic. Fortunately, this uneven performance does not occur with random data. The graph below shows how `qsort` performs on the three kinds of inputs we used for insertion sort: reverse-sorted, random, and equal-element sequences. As you can see, the number of operations for the equal-element sequences grows significantly faster than for the two other types.

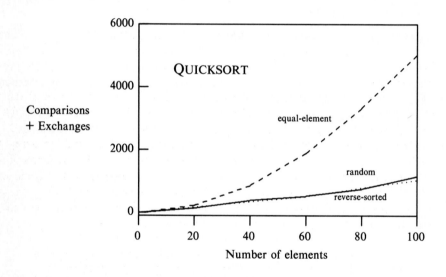

Exercise 7-4. Add counting statements to `qsort` to count the number of comparisons and exchanges. Does your data look like ours? □

Exercise 7-5. Instead of counting operations, time the program. Does the graph look the same? Try some larger examples. Does the graph still look the same? □

Heapsort

Basic idea. A *priority queue* is a data structure for storing and retrieving elements. There are two operations: insert a new element into the queue or extract the largest element from the queue. This suggests that a priority queue can be used to sort: first put all the elements into the queue and then remove them one at a time. Since the largest remaining element is removed at each step, the elements will be withdrawn in decreasing order. This technique underlies heapsort, a sorting algorithm devised by J. W. J. Williams and R. W. Floyd in the early 1960's.

Heapsort uses a data structure called a *heap* to maintain the priority queue. We can think of a heap as a binary tree with two properties:

1. The tree is balanced: the leaves appear on at most two different levels and the leaves on the bottom level (furthest from the root) are as far left as possible.

2. The tree is partially ordered: the element stored at each node is greater than or equal to the elements at its children.

Here is an example of a heap with ten elements:

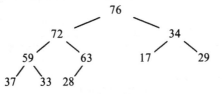

There are two important characteristics of a heap. The first is that if there are *n* nodes, then no path from the root to a leaf is longer than $\log_2 n$. The second is that the largest element is always at the root ("the top of the heap").

We don't need an explicit binary tree if we simulate a heap with an array A in which the elements at the nodes of the binary tree appear in the array in a "breadth-first" order. That is, the element at the root appears in A[1] and its children appear in A[2] and A[3]. In general, if a node is in A[i], then its children are in A[$2i$] and A[$2i+1$], or in just A[$2i$] if there is only one child. Thus, the array A for the elements shown above would contain:

A[1]	A[2]	A[3]	A[4]	A[5]	A[6]	A[7]	A[8]	A[9]	A[10]
76	72	34	59	63	17	29	37	33	28

The partially ordered property of the elements in a heap means that A[i] is greater than or equal to its children at A[$2i$] and A[$2i+1$], or to its child at A[$2i$] if there is only one child. If the elements of an array satisfy this condition, we say that the array has the "heap property."

Implementation. There are two phases to heapsort: building a heap and extracting the elements in order. Both phases use a function called heapify(A,i,j) to give the subarray A[i], A[i+1], ..., A[j] the heap property assuming A[i+1], ..., A[j] already has the property. The basic operation of heapify is to compare A[i] with its children. If A[i] has no children or is greater than its children, then heapify merely returns; otherwise, it swaps A[i] with its largest child and repeats the operation at that child.

In the first phase, heapsort transforms the array into a heap by calling heapify(A,i,n) for i going from $n/2$ down to 1.

At the start of the second phase i is set to n. Then three steps are executed repeatedly. First, A[1], the largest element in the heap, is exchanged with A[i], the rightmost element in the heap. Second, the size of the heap is reduced by one by decrementing i. These two steps have the effect of removing the largest element from the heap. Note that in doing so the last $n-i+1$ elements in the array are now in sorted order. Third, heapify(A, 1, $i-1$) is called to restore the heap property to the first $i-1$ elements of A.

These three steps are repeated until only a single element, the smallest, is left in the heap. Since the remaining elements in the array are in increasing order, the entire array is now sorted. During this process, the array looks like this:

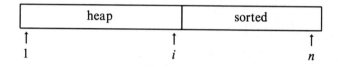

The elements in cells 1 through i of the array have the heap property; those in cells $i+1$ through n are the largest $n-i$ elements sorted in increasing order. Initially, $i=n$ and there is no sorted part.

Consider the array of elements shown above, which already has the heap property. In the first step of the second phase we exchange elements 76 and 28:

    28 72 34 59 63 17 29 37 33 ¦ 76

In the second step we decrement the heap size to nine. Then in the third step we restore the heap property to the first nine elements by moving 28 to its proper position in the heap by a sequence of swaps:

    72 63 34 59 28 17 29 37 33 ¦ 76

We can visualize this process as percolating the element 28 down a path in the binary tree from the root towards a leaf until the element is moved into a node all of whose children are less than or equal to 28:

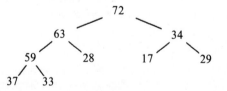

In the next iteration, the first step exchanges elements 72 and 33:

    33 63 34 59 28 17 29 37 ¦ 72 76

The second step decrements i to eight and the third propagates 33 to its proper position:

   63 59 34 37 28 17 29 33 ¦ 72 76

The next iteration begins by exchanging 63 and 33, and eventually produces the following configuration:

   59 37 34 33 28 17 29 ¦ 63 72 76

This process continues until the array is sorted.

The program below sorts its input into increasing order using this procedure. For reasons that will become apparent when we discuss profiling in the next section, we have enclosed most single-expression statements in braces.

```
# heapsort

    { A[NR] = $0 }

END { hsort(A, NR)
    for (i = 1; i <= NR; i++)
        { print A[i] }
    }

function hsort(A,n,   i) {
    for (i = int(n/2); i >= 1; i--)   # phase 1
        { heapify(A, i, n) }
    for (i = n; i > 1; i--) {          # phase 2
        { swap(A, 1, i) }
        { heapify(A, 1, i-1) }
    }
}
function heapify(A,left,right,   p,c) {
    for (p = left; (c = 2*p) <= right; p = c) {
        if (c < right && A[c+1] > A[c])
            { c++ }
        if (A[p] < A[c])
            { swap(A, c, p) }
    }
}
function swap(A,i,j,   t) {
    t = A[i]; A[i] = A[j]; A[j] = t
}
```

Performance. The total number of operations of hsort is proportional to $n \log n$, even in the worst case. Below we see the number of operations from running hsort on the same sequences we used to evaluate insertion sort and quicksort. Note that equal-element performance is better than quicksort.

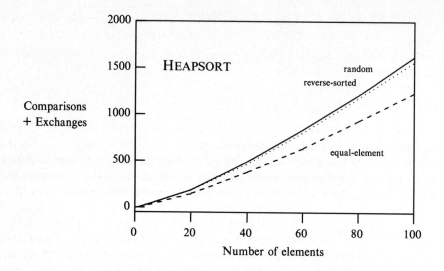

The next graph compares the performance of the three sorting algorithms of this section on random input data.

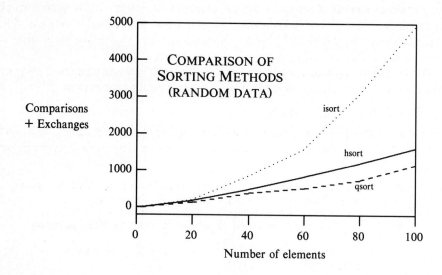

Recall that on random data the performance of isort is quadratic while that of hsort and qsort is $n\log n$. The graph clearly shows the importance of good algorithms: as the number of elements increases the difference in performance between the quadratic and the $n\log n$ programs widens dramatically.

Exercise 7-6. check always found that the output of isort was sorted. Will this be true of qsort and hsort? Would it be true when the input is just numbers, or just strings that don't look like numbers? ☐

7.2 Profiling

In the previous section, we evaluated the performance of a sorting program by counting the number of times certain operations were executed. Another effective way to evaluate the performance of a program is to profile it, that is, count the number of times each statement is executed. Many programming environments provide a tool, called a *profiler*, that will print a program with an execution count attached to each statement.

We don't have a profiler for awk, but in this section, we will show how to approximate one with two short programs. The first program, makeprof, makes a profiling version of an awk program by inserting counting and printing statements into the program. When the profiling program is run on some input, it counts the number of times each statement is executed and creates a file prof.cnts containing these counts. The second program, printprof, attaches the statement counts from prof.cnts to the original program.

To simplify the problem, we will only count the number of times each left brace is "executed" during the run of a program. Often this is good enough because every action and every compound statement is enclosed in braces. Any statement can be enclosed in braces, however, so we can obtain as precise an execution count as we wish by bracketing statements.

Here is the program makeprof that transforms an ordinary awk program into a profiling program. It inserts a counting statement of the form

```
_LBcnt[i]++;
```

after the first left brace appearing on any input line, and it adds a new END action that prints the values of these counters into prof.cnts, one count per line.

```
# makeprof - prepare profiling version of an awk program
#    usage:  awk -f makeprof awkprog >awkprog.p
#    running awk -f awkprog.p data creates a
#        file prof.cnts of statement counts for awkprog

{ if ($0 ~ /{/) sub(/{/, "{ _LBcnt[" ++_numLB "]++; ")
  print
}

END { printf("END { for (i = 1; i <= %d; i++)\n", _numLB)
      printf("\t\t print _LBcnt[i] > \"prof.cnts\"\n}\n")
    }
```

After running the profiling version of a program on some input data, we can attach the statement counts in `prof.cnts` to the original program with `printprof`:

```
# printprof - print profiling counts
#      usage:  awk -f printprof awkprog
#      prints awkprog with statement counts from prof.cnts

BEGIN { while (getline < "prof.cnts" > 0) cnt[++i] = $1 }
/{/    { printf("%5d", cnt[++j]) }
       { printf("\t%s\n", $0) }
```

As an example, consider profiling the `heapsort` program from the end of Section 7.1. To create the profiling version of this program, type the command line

```
awk -f makeprof heapsort >heapsort.p
```

The resulting program `heapsort.p` looks like this:

```
# heapsort

    { _LBcnt[1]++;  A[NR] = $0 }

END { _LBcnt[2]++;  hsort(A, NR)
    for (i = 1; i <= NR; i++)
        { _LBcnt[3]++;  print A[i] }
    }

function hsort(A,n,  i) { _LBcnt[4]++;
    for (i = int(n/2); i >= 1; i--)  # phase 1
        { _LBcnt[5]++;  heapify(A, i, n) }
    for (i = n; i > 1; i--) { _LBcnt[6]++;          # phase 2
        { _LBcnt[7]++;  swap(A, 1, i) }
        { _LBcnt[8]++;  heapify(A, 1, i-1) }
    }
}
function heapify(A,left,right,   p,c) { _LBcnt[9]++;
    for (p = left; (c = 2*p) <= right; p = c) { _LBcnt[10]++;
        if (c < right && A[c+1] > A[c])
            { _LBcnt[11]++;   c++ }
        if (A[p] < A[c])
            { _LBcnt[12]++;  swap(A, c, p) }
    }
}
function swap(A,i,j,   t) { _LBcnt[13]++;
    t = A[i]; A[i] = A[j]; A[j] = t
}
END { for (i = 1; i <= 13; i++)
        print _LBcnt[i] > "prof.cnts"
}
```

As you can see, thirteen counting statements have been inserted into the original program, along with a second END section that writes the counts into `prof.cnts`. Multiple END actions are treated as if they were just combined into one in the order in which they appear.

Now, suppose we run `heapsort.p` on 100 random integers. We can create a listing of the original program with the statement counts resulting from this run by typing the command line

```
awk -f printprof heapsort
```

The result is:

```
            # heapsort

100            { A[NR] = $0 }
  1         END { hsort(A, NR)
               for (i = 1; i <= NR; i++)
100                { print A[i] }
               }

  1         function hsort(A,n,   i) {
               for (i = int(n/2); i >= 1; i--)   # phase 1
 50                { heapify(A, i, n) }
 99            for (i = n; i > 1; i--) {   # phase 2
 99                { swap(A, 1, i) }
 99                { heapify(A, 1, i-1) }
               }
            }
149         function heapify(A,left,right,    p,c) {
521            for (p = left; (c = 2*p) <= right; p = c) {
                   if (c < right && A[c+1] > A[c])
232                    { c++ }
                   if (A[p] < A[c])
485                    { swap(A, c, p) }
               }
            }
584         function swap(A,i,j,    t) {
               t = A[i]; A[i] = A[j]; A[j] = t
            }
```

Simplicity, the greatest strength of this implementation, is also its greatest weakness. The program `makeprof` blindly inserts a counting statement after the first left brace it sees on each line; a more careful `makeprof` would not put counting statements inside string constants, regular expressions, or comments. It would also be nice to report execution times as well as counts, but that's not feasible with this approach.

Exercise 7-7. Modify the profiler so that counting statements will not be inserted into string constants, regular expressions, or comments. Will your version permit you to profile the profiler? □

Exercise 7-8. The profiler doesn't work if there is an `exit` statement in the END action. Why? Fix it. □

7.3   Topological Sorting

In a construction project, some jobs must be done before others can begin. We would like to list them so that each job precedes those that must be done after it. In a program library, a program a may call program h. Program h in turn may call programs d and e, and so on. We would like to order the programs so that a program appears before all the programs it calls. (The Unix program `lorder` does this.) These problems and others like them are instances of the problem of *topological sorting*: finding an ordering that satisfies a set of constraints of the form "x must come before y." In a topological sort any linear ordering that satisfies the partial order represented by the constraints is sufficient.

The constraints can be represented by a graph in which the nodes are labeled by the names, and there is an edge from node x to node y if x must come before y. The following graph is an example:

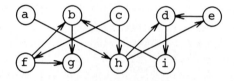

If a graph contains an edge from x to y, then x is called a *predecessor* of y, and y is a *successor* of x. Suppose the constraints come in the form of predecessor-successor pairs where each input line contains x and y representing an edge from node x to node y, as in this description of the graph above:

```
a    h
b    g
c    f
c    h
d    i
e    d
f    b
f    g
h    d
h    e
i    b
```

If there is an edge from x to y, then x must appear before y in the output. Given the input above, one possible output is the list

```
a c f h e d i b g
```

There are many other linear orders that contain the partial order depicted in the graph; another is

```
c a h e d i f b g
```

The problem of topological sorting is that of ordering the nodes of a graph so that all predecessors appear before their successors. Such an ordering is possible if and only if the graph does not contain a *cycle*, which is a sequence of edges that leads from a node back to itself. If the input graph contains a cycle, then we must say so and indicate that no linear ordering exists.

Breadth-First Topological Sort

There are many algorithms that can be used to sort a graph topologically. Perhaps the simplest is one that at each iteration removes from the graph a node with no predecessors. If all nodes can be removed from the graph this way, the sequence in which the nodes are removed is a topological sort of the graph. In the graph above, we could begin by removing node a and the edge that comes from it. Then we could remove node c, then nodes f and h in either order, and so on.

Our implementation uses a first-in, first-out data structure called a *queue* to sequence the processing of nodes with no predecessors in a "breadth-first" manner. After all the data has been read in, a loop counts the nodes and places all nodes with no predecessors on the queue. A second loop removes the node at the front of the queue, prints its name, and decrements the predecessor count of each of its successors. If the predecessor count of any of its successors becomes zero, those successors are put on the back of the queue. When the front catches up to the back and all nodes have been considered, the job is done. But, if some nodes are never put on the queue, those nodes are involved in cycles and no topological sort is possible. When no cycles are present, the sequence of nodes printed is a topological sort.

The first three statements of tsort read the predecessor-successor pairs from the input and construct a successor-list data structure like this:

node	pcnt	scnt	slist
a	0	1	h
b	2	1	g
c	0	2	f, h
d	2	1	i
e	1	1	d
f	1	2	b, g
g	2	0	
h	2	2	d, e
i	1	1	b

The arrays pcnt and scnt keep track of the number of predecessors and successors for each node; slist[x,i] gives the node that is the i-th successor of node x. The first line creates an element of pcnt if it is not already present.

```
# tsort - topological sort of a graph
#    input:  predecessor-successor pairs
#    output: linear order, predecessors first

    { if (!($1 in pcnt))
          pcnt[$1] = 0                # put $1 in pcnt
      pcnt[$2]++                      # count predecessors of $2
      slist[$1, ++scnt[$1]] = $2 # add $2 to successors of $1
    }
END { for (node in pcnt) {
          nodecnt++
          if (pcnt[node] == 0)   # if it has no predecessors
              q[++back] = node   # queue node
      }
      for (front = 1; front <= back; front++) {
          printf(" %s", node = q[front])
          for (i = 1; i <= scnt[node]; i++)
              if (--pcnt[slist[node, i]] == 0)
                  # queue s if it has no more predecessors
                  q[++back] = slist[node, i]
      }
      if (back != nodecnt)
          print "\nerror: input contains a cycle"
      printf("\n")
    }
```

The implementation of a queue is especially easy in awk: it's just an array with two subscripts, one for the front and one for the back.

Exercise 7-9. Fix tsort so it can handle isolated nodes in the graph. □

Depth-First Search

We will construct one more topological sort program in order to illustrate an important technique called depth-first search, which can also be used to solve many other graph problems, including one that arises in the Unix utility make. Depth-first search is another method of visiting the nodes of a graph, even one with cycles, in a systematic manner. In its purest form, it is just a recursive procedure:

> dfs(*node*):
> > mark *node* visited
> > for all unvisited successors *s* of *node* do
> > > dfs(*s*)

The reason the technique is called depth-first search is that it starts at a node, then visits an unvisited successor of that node, then an unvisited successor of that successor, and so on, plunging as deeply into the graph as quickly as it can. Once there are no unvisited successors of a node, the search retreats to the predecessor of that node and visits another of its unvisited successors in a depth-first search.

Consider the following graph. If it starts at node 1, a depth-first search will visit nodes 1, 2, 3, and 4. At that point, if it starts with another unvisited node such as 5, it will then visit nodes 5, 6, and 7. If it starts at a different place, however, a different sequence of visits will be made.

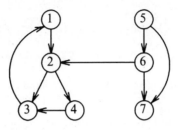

Depth-first search is useful for finding cycles. An edge like (3,1) that goes from a node to a previously visited ancestor is called a *back edge*. Since a back edge identifies a cycle, to find cycles all we need to do is find back edges. The following function will test whether a graph, stored as a successor-list data structure like that in `tsort`, contains a cycle reachable from `node`:

```
# dfs - depth-first search for cycles

function dfs(node,      i, s) {
    visited[node] = 1
    for (i = 1; i <= scnt[node]; i++)
        if (visited[s = slist[node, i]] == 0)
            dfs(s)
        else if (visited[s] == 1)
            print "cycle with back edge (" node ", " s ")"
    visited[node] = 2
}
```

This function uses an array `visited` to determine whether a node has been traversed. Initially, `visited[x]` is 0 for all nodes. Entering a node x for the first time, `dfs` sets `visited[x]` to 1, and leaving x for the last time it sets `visited[x]` to 2. During the traversal, `dfs` uses `visited` to determine whether a node y is an ancestor of the current node (and hence previously visited), in which case `visited[y]` is 1, or whether y has been previously visited, in which case `visited[y]` is 2.

Depth-First Topological Sort

The function `dfs` can easily be turned into a node-sorting procedure. If it prints the name of each node once the search from that node is completed, it will generate a list of nodes that is a reverse topological sort, provided again there are no cycles in the graph. The program `rtsort` prints the reverse of a topological sort of a graph, given a sequence of predecessor-successor pairs as input. It applies depth-first search to every node with no predecessors. The data structure is the same as that in `tsort`.

```
# rtsort - reverse topological sort
#    input:  predecessor-successor pairs
#    output: linear order, successors first

    { if (!($1 in pcnt))
          pcnt[$1] = 0                # put $1 in pcnt
      pcnt[$2]++                      # count predecessors of $2
      slist[$1, ++scnt[$1]] = $2 # add $2 to successors of $1
    }

END { for (node in pcnt) {
          nodecnt++
          if (pcnt[node] == 0)
              rtsort(node)
      }
      if (pncnt != nodecnt)
          print "error: input contains a cycle"
      printf("\n")
    }

function rtsort(node,      i, s) {
    visited[node] = 1
    for (i = 1; i <= scnt[node]; i++)
        if (visited[s = slist[node, i]] == 0)
            rtsort(s)
        else if (visited[s] == 1)
            printf("error: nodes %s and %s are in a cycle\n",
                s, node)
    visited[node] = 2
    printf(" %s", node)
    pncnt++     # count nodes printed
}
```

Applied to the predecessor-successor pairs at the beginning of this section, `rtsort` would print

```
    g b i d e h a f c
```

Notice that this algorithm detects some cycles explicitly by finding a back edge, while it detects other cycles only implicitly, by failing to print all the nodes, as in this graph:

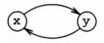

Exercise 7-10. Modify `rtsort` to print its output in the usual order, predecessors first. Can you achieve the same effect without modifying `rtsort`? □

7.4   Make: A File Updating Program

A large program may consist of declarations and subprograms that are stored in scores of separate files, with an involved sequence of processing steps to create a running version. A complex document (like this chapter) may consist of graphs and diagrams stored in multiple files, programs to be run and tested, and then interdependent operations to make a printed copy. An automatic updating facility is an invaluable tool for processing such systems of files with a minimum of human and machine time. This section develops a rudimentary updating program, patterned after the Unix make command, that is based on the depth-first search technique of the previous section.

To use the updater, one must explicitly describe what the components of the system are, how they depend upon one another, and what commands are needed to construct them. We'll assume these dependencies and commands are stored in a file, called a makefile, that contains a sequence of rules of the form:

$$name: \quad t_1 \; t_2 \; ... \; t_n$$
$$commands$$

The first line of a rule is a dependency relation that states that the program or file *name* depends on the targets t_1, t_2, ..., t_n where each t_i is a filename or another *name*. Following each dependency relation may be one or more lines of *commands* that list the commands necessary to generate *name*. Here is an example of a makefile for a small program with two C files and a yacc grammar file, a typical program-development application.

```
prog:      a.o b.o c.o
           cc a.o b.o c.o -ly -o prog
a.o:       prog.h a.c
           cc -c prog.h a.c
b.o:       prog.h b.c
           cc -c prog.h b.c
c.o:       c.c
           cc -c c.c
c.c:       c.y
           yacc c.y
           mv y.tab.c c.c
print:
           pr prog.h a.c b.c c.y
```

The first line states that prog depends on the target files a.o, b.o and c.o. The second line says that prog is generated by using the C compiler command cc to link a.o, b.o, c.o, and a library into the file prog. The next rule (third line) states that a.o depends on the targets prog.h and a.c and is created by compiling these targets; b.o is the same. The file c.o depends on c.c, which in turn depends on c.y, which has to be processed by the yacc parser generator. Finally, the name print does not depend on any target; by convention, for targetless names make will always perform the associated action, in this case printing all the source files with the command pr.

The dependency relations in the `makefile` can be represented by a graph in which there is an edge from node x to node y whenever there is a dependency rule with x on the left side and y one of the targets on the right. For a rule with no targets, a successorless node with the name on the left is created. For the `makefile` above, we have the following dependency graph:

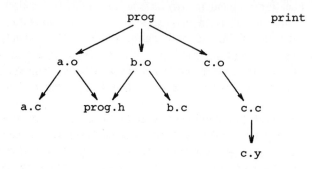

We say that x is *older* than y if y was changed after x was last changed. To keep track of ages, we will attach to each x an integer `age[x]` that represents how long ago x was last modified. The larger the age, the older the file: x is older than y if `age[x]` $\geq$ `age[y]`.

If we use the dependency relation

```
n: a b c
```

we update n by first updating a, b and c, which may in turn require further updates. If any of the targets is neither a name in the `makefile` nor an existing file, we report the error and quit. Otherwise, we next examine the ages of the targets, and if at least one is newer than n (that is, if n is older than something it depends on), we execute the commands associated with this dependency relation. After executing the commands, we recompute the ages of all objects. With a dependency relation like

```
print:
      pr prog.h a.c b.c c.y
```

that is, one with no targets, we always execute the command associated with this rule and recompute all ages.

The program `make` takes a *name* as an argument and updates *name* using the following algorithm:

1. It finds the rule for *name* in the `makefile` and recursively updates the targets t_1, t_2, ..., t_n on the right side of the dependency relation for *name*. If for some i, t_i is not a name and file t_i does not exist, `make` aborts the update.

2. If, after updating all the t_i's, the current version of *name* is older than one or

more of the t_i's, or if *name* has no targets, make executes the command lines following the dependency relation for *name*.

In essentially the same manner as in the previous section, make constructs a dependency graph from the dependency relations in the makefile. It uses the Unix command

```
ls -t
```

to order the files (newest first) by the time at which each file was last modified. Each filename is entered into the array age and given a time that is its rank in this ordering; the oldest file has the largest rank. If a name is not a file in the current directory, make sets its time to a large value, thus making it very old indeed.

Finally, make uses the depth-first search procedure of the last section to traverse the dependency graph. At node n, make traverses the successors of n; if any successor becomes younger than the current age of n, make executes the commands for n and computes a new set of ages. If make discovers that the dependency relation for a name is cyclic, it says so and aborts the update.

To illustrate how make works, suppose we type the command line

```
make prog
```

for the first time. Then make will execute the following sequence of commands:

```
cc -c prog.h a.c
cc -c prog.h b.c
yacc c.y
mv y.tab.c c.c
cc -c c.c
cc a.o b.o c.o -ly -o prog
```

Now if we make a change to b.c and again type

```
make prog
```

make will only execute

```
cc -c prog.h b.c
cc a.o b.o c.o -ly -o prog
```

Because the other files have not changed since the last time prog was created, make does not process them. Finally, if we again say

```
make prog
```

the result is

```
prog is up to date
```

because nothing has to be done.

```
# make - maintain dependencies

BEGIN {
    while (getline <"makefile" > 0)
        if ($0 ~ /^[A-Za-z]/) {    #  $1: $2 $3 ...
            sub(/:/, "")
            if (++names[nm = $1] > 1)
                error(nm " is multiply defined")
            for (i = 2; i <= NF; i++) # remember targets
                slist[nm, ++scnt[nm]] = $i
        } else if ($0 ~ /^\t/)             # remember cmd for
            cmd[nm] = cmd[nm] $0 "\n" #    current name
        else if (NF > 0)
            error("illegal line in makefile: " $0)
    ages()        # compute initial ages
    if (ARGV[1] in names) {
        if (update(ARGV[1]) == 0)
            print ARGV[1] " is up to date"
    } else
        error(ARGV[1] " is not in makefile")
}

function ages(        f,n,t) {
    for (t = 1; ("ls -t" | getline f) > 0; t++)
        age[f] = t    # all existing files get an age
    close("ls -t")
    for (n in names)
        if (!(n in age))    # if n has not been created
            age[n] = 9999  # make n really old
}
function update(n,    changed,i,s) {
    if (!(n in age)) error(n " does not exist")
    if (!(n in names)) return 0
    changed = 0
    visited[n] = 1
    for (i = 1; i <= scnt[n]; i++) {
        if (visited[s = slist[n, i]] == 0) update(s)
        else if (visited[s] == 1)
            error(s " and " n " are circularly defined")
        if (age[s] <= age[n]) changed++
    }
    visited[n] = 2
    if (changed || scnt[n] == 0) {
        printf("%s", cmd[n])
        system(cmd[n])  # execute cmd associated with n
        ages()          # recompute all ages
        age[n] = 0      # make n very new
        return 1
    }
    return 0
}
function error(s) { print "error: " s; exit }
```

Exercise 7-11. How many times is the function `ages` executed on the example? □

Exercise 7-12. Add some parameter or macro substitution mechanism so rules can be easily changed. □

Exercise 7-13. Add implicit rules for common updating operations; for example, `.c` files are processed by `cc` to make `.o` files. How can you represent the implicit rules so they can be changed by users? □

7.5 Summary

This chapter may have more of the flavor of a basic course in algorithms than instruction in awk. The algorithms are genuinely useful, however, and we hope that in addition you have seen something of how awk can be used to support experimentation with programs.

Scaffolding is one of the lessons. It often takes no more time to write a small program to generate and control testing or debugging than it does to perform a single test, but the scaffolding can be used over and over to do a much more thorough job.

The other aspect is more conventional, though it bears repeating. Awk is often just right for extracting data from the output of some program and massaging it for another; for example, that is how we converted sorting measurements into `grap` input and how we folded statement counts into a profile.

Bibliographic Notes

Our quicksort, heapsort, and topological sort programs are borrowed from Jon Bentley, as is the inspiration for the scaffolding and profiling programs. Bentley's *Programming Pearls* columns in *Communications of the ACM*, June and July, 1985, are good further reading. For an extensive discussion and analysis of sorting and searching algorithms see D. E. Knuth's *The Art of Computer Programming*, Volume 3: Sorting and Searching (Addison-Wesley, 1973), or Aho, Hopcroft, and Ullman's *The Design and Analysis of Computer Algorithms* (Addison-Wesley, 1974).

The Unix program `make` is originally due to Stu Feldman; it was first described in *Software—Practice and Experience*, April, 1979. For more discussion of `make` and its behavior, see the article "Side-effects in Automatic File Updating" by W. Miller and E. Myers in *Software—Practice and Experience*, September, 1986.

8   EPILOG

By now the reader should be a reasonably adept awk user, or at least no longer an awkward beginner. As you have studied the examples and written some of your own, you have probably wondered why awk programs are the way they are, and perhaps wanted to make them better.

The first part of this chapter describes a little history, and discusses the strong and weak points of awk as a programming language. The second part explores the performance of awk programs, and suggests some ways of reformulating problems that have become too large for a single program.

8.1   AWK as a Language

We began working on awk in 1977. At that time the Unix programs that searched files (grep and sed) only had regular expression patterns, and the only actions were substitution and printing the whole line. There were no fields and no numeric operations. Our goal, as we remember it, was to create a pattern-scanning language that would understand fields, one with patterns to match fields and actions to manipulate them. Initially, we just wanted to do transformations on data, to scan the inputs of programs for validation, and to process the outputs to generate reports or to rearrange them for input to other programs.

The 1977 version had only a few built-in variables and predefined functions. It was designed for writing short programs like those in Chapter 1. Furthermore, it was designed to be used by our immediate colleagues with little instruction, so for regular expressions we used the familiar notation of lex and egrep, and for the other expressions and statements we used the syntax of C.

Our model was that an invocation would be one or two lines long, typed in and used immediately. Defaults were chosen to match this style. In particular, white space as the default field separator, implicit initializations, and no type declarations for variables were choices that made it possible to write one-liners. We, being the authors, "knew" how the language was supposed to be used, and so we only wrote one-liners.

Awk quickly spread to other groups and users pushed hard on the language. We were surprised at how rapidly awk became popular as a general-purpose programming language; our first reaction to a program that didn't fit on one page was shock and amazement. What had happened was that many people restricted their use of the computer to the shell (the command language) and to awk. Rather than writing in a "real" programming language, they were stretching the tools they liked.

The idea of having each variable maintain both a string and a numeric representation of its value, and use the form appropriate to the context, was an experiment. The goal was to make it possible to write short programs using only one set of operators, but have them work correctly in the face of ambiguity about strings and numbers. The goal was largely met, but there are still occasional surprises for the unwary. The rules in Chapter 2 for resolving ambiguous cases evolved from user experience.

Associative arrays were inspired by SNOBOL4 tables, although they are not as general. Awk was born on a slow machine with a small memory, and the properties of arrays were a result of that environment. Restricting subscripts to be strings is one manifestation, as is the restriction to a single dimension (even with syntactic sugar). A more general implementation would allow multi-dimensional arrays, or at least allow arrays to be array elements.

Major facilities were added to awk in 1985, largely in response to user demand. These additions included dynamic regular expressions, new built-in variables and functions, multiple input streams, and, most importantly, user-defined functions.

The new substitution functions, match, and dynamic regular expressions provided useful capabilities with a only small increase in complexity for users.

Before getline the only kind of input was the implicit input loop implied by the pattern-action statements. That was fairly constricting. In the original language, a program like the form-letter generator that has more than one source of input required setting a flag variable or some similar trick to read the sources. In the new language, multiple inputs can be naturally read with getline's in the BEGIN section. On the other hand, getline is overloaded, and its syntax doesn't match the other expressions. Part of the problem is that getline needs to return what it reads, and also some indication of success or failure.

The implementation of user-defined functions was a compromise. The chief difficulties arose from the initial design of awk. We did not have, or want, declarations in the language. One result is the peculiar way of declaring local variables as extra formal parameters. Besides looking strange, this is error prone in large programs. In addition, the absence of an explicit concatenation operator, an advantage for short programs, now requires the opening parenthesis of a function call to follow the function name with no intervening blanks. Nevertheless, the new facilities made awk significantly better for larger applications.

8.2 Performance

In a way, awk is seductive — it is often quite easy to write a program that does what you want, and for modest amounts of data, is fast enough, especially when the program itself is still undergoing changes.

But as a working awk program is applied to bigger and bigger files, it gets slower and slower. Rationally this must be so, but waiting for your results may be too much to bear. There are no simple solutions, but this section contains suggestions that might be helpful.

When programs take too long to run, there are several things to think about doing, besides just putting up with it. First, it is possible that the program can be made faster, either by a better algorithm or by replacing some frequently executed expensive construction with a cheaper one. You have already seen in Chapter 7 how much difference a good algorithm can make — the difference between a linear algorithm and a quadratic one grows dramatically even with modest increases in data. Second, you can use other, faster programs along with awk, restricting awk's role. Third, you can rewrite the entire program in some other language.

Before you can improve the behavior of a program, you need to understand where the time is going. Even in languages where each operation is close to the underlying hardware, people's initial estimates of where time is being spent are notoriously unreliable. Such estimates are even trickier in awk, since many of its operations do not correspond to conventional machine operations. Among these are pattern matching, field splitting, string concatenation, and substitution. The instructions that awk executes to implement these operations vary from machine to machine, and so do their relative costs in awk programs.

Awk has no built-in tools for timing. Thus it's up to the user to understand what's expensive and what's cheap in the local environment. The easiest way to do this is to make differential measurements of various constructs. For example, how much does it cost to read a line or increment a variable? We made measurements on a variety of computers, ranging from a PC to a mainframe. We ran three programs on an input file of 10,000 lines (500,000 characters), as well as the Unix command wc for comparison. The results are summarized in this table:

PROGRAM	AT&T 6300+	DEC VAX 11-750	AT&T 3B2/600	SUN-3	DEC VAX 8550
END { print NR }	30	17.4	5.9	4.6	1.6
{n++}; END {print n}	45	24.4	8.4	6.5	2.4
{ i = NF }	59	34.8	12.5	9.3	3.3
wc command	30	8.2	2.9	3.3	1.0

The first program takes 1.6 seconds on a DEC VAX 8550; this means that it takes 0.16 milliseconds to read a line. The second program shows that it takes another 0.08 milliseconds to increment a variable. The third program shows that it takes 0.33 milliseconds to split each line into fields. By contrast, it takes one second to count the 10,000 lines with a C program (the Unix program wc), or 0.1 milliseconds per line.

Similar measurements show that a string comparison like $1=="xxx" costs about the same as the regular expression match $1~/xxx/. The cost of matching a regular expression is just about independent of its complexity, however, while a compound comparison costs more as it gets more complicated. Dynamic regular expressions can be more expensive, since it may be necessary to re-create a recognizer for each test.

Concatenating lots of strings is expensive:

```
print $1 " " $2 " " $3 " " $4 " " $5
```

takes twice as long as

```
print $1, $2, $3, $4, $5
```

As we hinted earlier, arrays have complex behavior. As long as there are not too many elements in an array, accessing an element takes a constant amount of time. After that the amount of time increases roughly linearly with the number of elements. If there are a very large number of elements, the operating system may get involved, looking for memory to store things in. Thus, each element in a big array is more expensive than an element in a little array. This is worth remembering if you are trying to store a large file in an array.

The second line of attack is to restructure the computation so that some of the work is done by other programs. Throughout this book, we made extensive use of the system sort command, for example, rather than writing our own sort in awk. If you have to search a big file to isolate a small amount of data, use grep or egrep for the searching and awk for the processing. If there are a large number of substitutions (for example, the cross-reference program of Chapter 5), you might use a stream editor like sed for that part. In other words, break the job into separate pieces, and apply the most appropriate tool to each piece.

The last resort is to rewrite the offending program in some other language. The guiding principle is to replace the useful built-in features of awk with subroutines, and otherwise use much the same structure as the original program. Don't attempt to simulate exactly what awk does. Instead provide just enough for the problem at hand. A useful exercise is to write a small library that provides field-splitting, associative arrays, and regular expression matching; in languages like C that do not provide dynamic strings, you will also want some routines that allocate and free strings conveniently. With this library in hand, converting an awk program into something that will run faster is quite feasible.

Awk makes easy many things that are hard in conventional languages, by providing features like pattern matching, field splitting, and associative arrays. The penalty paid is that an awk program using these features, however easy to write, is not as efficient as a carefully written C program for the same task. Frequently efficiency is not critical, and so awk is both convenient to use, and fast enough.

When awk isn't fast enough, it is important to measure the pieces of the job, to see where the time is going. The relative costs of various operations differ from machine to machine, but the measurement techniques can be used on any machine. Finally, even though it is less convenient to program in lower-level languages, the same principles of timing and understanding have to be applied, or else the new program will be both harder to write and less efficient.

8.3 Conclusion

Awk is not a solution to every programming problem, but it's an indispensable part of a programmer's toolbox, especially on Unix, where easy connection of tools is a way of life. Although the larger examples in the book might give a different impression, most awk programs are short and simple and do tasks the language was originally meant for: counting things, converting data from one form to another, adding up numbers, extracting information for reports.

For tasks like these, where program development time is more important than run time, awk is hard to beat. The implicit input loop and the pattern-action paradigm simplify and often entirely eliminate control flow. Field splitting parses the most common forms of input, while numbers and strings and the coercions between them handle the most common data types. Associative arrays provide both conventional array storage and the much richer possibilities of arbitrary subscripts. Regular expressions are a uniform notation for describing patterns of text. Default initialization and the absence of declarations shorten programs.

What we did not anticipate were the less conventional applications. For example, the transition from "not programming" to "programming" is quite gradual: the absence of the syntactic baggage of conventional languages like C or Pascal makes awk easy enough to learn that it has been the first language for a surprising number of people.

The features added in 1985, especially the ability to define functions, have led to a variety of unexpected applications, like small database systems and compilers for little languages. In many cases, awk is used for a prototype, an experiment to demonstrate feasibility and to play with features and user interfaces, although sometimes the awk program remains the production version. Awk has even been used for software engineering courses, because it's possible to experiment with designs much more readily than with larger languages.

Of course, one must be wary of going too far — any tool can be pushed beyond its limits — but many people have found awk to be valuable for a wide range of problems. We hope we have suggested ways in which awk might be useful to you as well.

Bibliographic Notes

The original version of awk was described by the authors in "AWK—a pattern scanning and processing language," which appeared in *Software—Practice and Experience*, April 1979. This article also contains a technical discussion of the design of the language.

Much of the syntax of awk is derived from C, described in *The C Programming Language*, by B. W. Kernighan and D. M. Ritchie (Prentice-Hall, 1978). The regular expressions used in the programs `egrep`, `lex`, and `sed` are described in Section 2 of *The Unix Programmer's Manual*. Chapter 3 of *Compilers: Principles, Techniques, and Tools*, by Aho, Sethi, and Ullman (Addison-Wesley, 1986) contains a description of the regular expression pattern-matching technique used in the new version of awk.

You might find it interesting to compare awk with similar languages. Certainly the patriarch of the family is SNOBOL4, described in *The SNOBOL4 Programming Language*, by R. Griswold, J. Poage, and I. Polonsky (Prentice-Hall, 1971). Although SNOBOL4 suffers from an unstructured input language, it is powerful and expressive. ICON, described in *The ICON Programming Language* by R. Griswold and M. Griswold (Prentice-Hall, 1983), is a lineal descendant of SNOBOL, with a nicer syntax and a better integration of the pattern facilities with the rest of the language. The REXX command interpreter language for IBM systems is another language in the same spirit, although with more emphasis on its role as a shell or command interpreter; see, for example, M. F. Cowlishaw's *The REXX Language* (Prentice-Hall, 1985).

A AWK SUMMARY

This appendix contains a summary of the awk language. In syntactic rules, components enclosed in brackets [...] are optional.

Command-line

       awk [-F*s*] *'program' optional list of filenames*
       awk [-F*s*] -f *progfile optional list of filenames*

The option -F*s* sets the field separator variable FS to *s*. If there are no filenames, the standard input is read. A filename can be of the form *var=text*, in which case it is treated as an assignment of *text* to the variable *var*, performed at the time when that argument would be accessed as a file.

AWK programs

An awk program is a sequence of pattern-action statements and function definitions. A pattern-action statement has the form:

       pattern   { *action* }

An omitted pattern matches all input lines; an omitted action prints a matched line.
A function definition has the form:

       function *name(parameter-list)* { *statement* }

Pattern-action statements and function definitions are separated by newlines or semicolons and can be intermixed.

Patterns

       BEGIN
       END
       expression
       /regular expression/
       pattern && *pattern*
       pattern ¦¦ *pattern*
       !*pattern*
       (*pattern*)
       pattern, *pattern*

The last pattern is a range pattern, which cannot be part of another pattern. Similarly, BEGIN and END do not combine with other patterns.

Actions

An action is a sequence of statements of the following kinds:

```
break
continue
delete array-element
do statement while (expression)
exit [expression]
expression
if (expression) statement [else statement]
input-output statement
for (expression; expression; expression) statement
for (variable in array) statement
next
return [expression]
while (expression) statement
{ statements }
```

A semicolon by itself denotes the empty statement. In an `if-else` statement, the first *statement* must be terminated by a semicolon or enclosed in braces if it appears on the same line as `else`. Similarly, in a `do` statement, *statement* must be terminated by a semicolon or enclosed in braces if it appears on the same line as `while`.

Program format

Statements are separated by newlines or semicolons or both. Blank lines may be inserted before or after any statement, pattern-action statement, or function definition. Spaces and tabs may be inserted around operators and operands. A long statement may be broken by a backslash. In addition, a statement may be broken without a backslash after a comma, left brace, &&, ¦ ¦, do, else, and the right parenthesis in an `if` or `for` statement. A comment beginning with # can be put at the end of any line.

Input-output

`close(expr)`	close file or pipe denoted by *expr*
`getline`	set $0 from next input record; set NF, NR, FNR
`getline <file`	set $0 from next record of *file*; set NF
`getline var`	set *var* from next input record; set NR, FNR
`getline var <file`	set *var* from next record of *file*
`print`	print current record
`print expr-list`	print expressions in *expr-list*
`print expr-list >file`	print expressions on *file*
`printf fmt, expr-list`	format and print
`printf fmt, expr-list >file`	format and print on *file*
`system(cmd-line)`	execute command *cmd-line*, return status

The *expr-list* following `print` and the *fmt, expr-list* following `printf` may be parenthesized. In `print` and `printf`, >>*file* appends to the *file*, and ¦ *command* writes on a pipe. Similarly, *command* ¦ `getline` pipes into `getline`. The function `getline` returns 0 on end of file, and −1 on error.

Printf format conversions

These conversions are recognized in `printf` and `sprintf` statements.

%c	ASCII character
%d	decimal number
%e	[-]d.ddddddE[+-]dd
%f	[-]ddd.dddddd
%g	e or f conversion, whichever is shorter, with nonsignificant zeros suppressed
%o	unsigned octal number
%s	string
%x	unsigned hexadecimal number
%%	print a %; no argument is converted

Additional parameters may lie between the % and the control letter:

-	left-justify expression in its field
width	pad field to this width as needed; leading 0 pads with zeros
.*prec*	maximum string width or digits to right of decimal point

Built-in variables

The following built-in variables can be used in any expression:

ARGC	number of command-line arguments
ARGV	array of command-line arguments (ARGV[0..ARGC-1])
FILENAME	name of current input file
FNR	input record number in current file
FS	input field separator (default blank)
NF	number of fields in current input record
NR	input record number since beginning
OFMT	output format for numbers (default "%.6g")
OFS	output field separator (default blank)
ORS	output record separator (default newline)
RLENGTH	length of string matched by regular expression in `match`
RS	input record separator (default newline)
RSTART	beginning position of string matched by `match`
SUBSEP	separator for array subscripts of form [$i,j,...$] (default "\034")

ARGC and ARGV include the name of the invoking program (usually `awk`) but not the program arguments or options. RSTART is also the value returned by `match`.

The current input record is named $0. The fields in the current input record are named $1, $2, ..., $NF.

Built-in string functions

In the following string functions, s and t represent strings, r a regular expression, and i and n integers.

An & in the replacement string s in `sub` and `gsub` is replaced by the matched string; \& yields a literal ampersand.

gsub(r,s,t)	globally substitute s for each substring of t matched by r, return number of substitutions; if t is omitted, $0 is used
index(s,t)	return the index of t in s, or 0 if s does not contain t
length(s)	return the length of s
match(s,r)	return index of where s matches r or 0 if there is no match; set RSTART and RLENGTH
split(s,a,fs)	split s into array a on fs, return number of fields; if fs is omitted, FS is used in its place
sprintf(fmt, expr-list)	return expr-list formatted according to fmt
sub(r,s,t)	like gsub except only the first matched substring is replaced
substr(s,i,n)	return the n-character substring of s starting at i; if n is omitted, return the suffix of s starting at i

Built-in arithmetic functions

atan2(y,x)	arctangent of y/x in radians in the range $-\pi$ to π
cos(x)	cosine (angle in radians)
exp(x)	exponential e^x
int(x)	truncate to integer
log(x)	natural logarithm
rand()	pseudo-random number r, $0 \leqslant r < 1$
sin(x)	sine (angle in radians)
sqrt(x)	square root
srand(x)	set new seed for random number generator; uses time of day if no x given

Expression operators (increasing in precedence)

Expressions may be combined with the following operators:

= += -= *= /= %= ^=	assignment
? :	conditional expression
¦ ¦	logical OR
&&	logical AND
in	array membership
~ !~	regular expression match, negated match
< <= > >= != ==	relationals
	string concatenation (no explicit operator)
+ -	add, subtract
* / %	multiply, divide, mod
+ - !	unary plus, unary minus, logical NOT
^	exponentiation
++ --	increment, decrement (prefix and postfix)
$	field

All operators are left associative, except assignment, ?:, and ^, which are right associative. Any expression may be parenthesized.

Regular expressions

The regular expression metacharacters are

    \ ^ \$. [ ] | ( ) * + ?

The following table summarizes regular expressions and the strings they match:

c	matches the nonmetacharacter c
\c	matches the escape sequence or literal character c
^	matches the beginning of a string
\$	matches the end of a string
.	matches any single character
[abc...]	character class: matches any of abc...
[^abc...]	negated class: matches any single character but abc...
$r_1	r_2$	alternation: matches any string matched by r_1 or r_2
$(r_1)(r_2)$	concatenation: matches xy where r_1 matches x and r_2 matches y
$(r)*$	matches zero or more consecutive strings matched by r
$(r)+$	matches one or more consecutive strings matched by r
$(r)?$	matches the null string or one string matched by r
(r)	grouping: matches the same strings as r

The operators are listed in increasing precedence. Redundant parentheses in regular expressions may be omitted as long as the precedence of operators is respected.

Escape sequences

These sequences have special meanings in strings and regular expressions.

\b	backspace
\f	formfeed
\n	newline
\r	carriage return
\t	tab
\ddd	octal value ddd, where ddd is 1 to 3 digits between 0 and 7
\c	any other character c literally, e.g., \" for " and \\ for \

Limits

Any particular implementation of awk enforces some limits. Here are typical values:

    100 fields
    3000 characters per input record
    3000 characters per output record
    1024 characters per field
    3000 characters per `printf` string
    400 characters maximum literal string
    400 characters in character class
    15 open files
    1 pipe
    double-precision floating point

Numbers are limited to what can be represented on the local machine, e.g., $10^{-38}..10^{38}$; numbers outside this range will have string values only.

Initialization, comparison, and type coercion

Each variable and field can potentially be a string or a number or both at any time. When a variable is set by an assignment

```
var = expr
```

its type is set to that of the expression. ("Assignment" includes +=, -=, etc.) An arithmetic expression is of type number, a concatenation is of type string, and so on. If the assignment is a simple copy, as in v1 = v2, then the type of v1 is set to that of v2.

In comparisons, if both operands are numeric, the comparison is made numerically. Otherwise, operands are coerced to string if necessary, and the comparison is made on strings. The type of any expression can be coerced to numeric by subterfuges such as

```
expr + 0
```

and to string by

```
expr ""
```

(i.e., concatenation with a null string). The numeric value of an arbitrary string is the numeric value of its numeric prefix.

Uninitialized variables have the numeric value 0 and the string value "". Accordingly, if x is uninitialized,

```
if (x) ...
```

is false, and

```
if (!x) ...
if (x == 0) ...
if (x == "") ...
```

are all true. But note that

```
if (x == "0") ...
```

is false.

The type of a field is determined by context when possible; for example,

```
$1++
```

implies that $1 must be coerced to numeric if necessary, and

```
$1 = $1 "," $2
```

implies that $1 and $2 will be coerced to strings if necessary.

In contexts where types cannot be reliably determined, e.g.,

```
if ($1 == $2) ...
```

the type of each field is determined on input. All fields are strings; in addition, each field that contains only a number is also considered numeric.

Fields that are explicitly null have the string value ""; they are not numeric. Nonexistent fields (i.e., fields past NF) and $0 for blank lines are treated this way too.

As it is for fields, so it is for array elements created by split.

Mentioning a variable in an expression causes it to exist, with the values 0 and "" as described above. Thus, if arr[i] does not currently exist,

```
if (arr[i] == "") ...
```

causes it to exist with the value "" and thus the if is satisfied. The test

```
if (i in arr) ...
```

determines if arr[i] exists without the side effect of creating it.

B   ANSWERS TO SELECTED EXERCISES

Exercise 3-1. An easy way to ignore blank lines is to replace the first line of sum3 by

```
nfld == 0 && NF > 0 { nfld = NF
```

□

Exercise 3-3. Without the test, sums of nonnumeric columns get accumulated, but not printed. Having the test avoids the possibility that something will go wrong (like overflow) while accumulating the useless sums. There is no significant effect on speed. □

Exercise 3-4. This problem is easily handled with an associative array:

```
        { total[$1] += $2 }
END { for (x in total) print x, total[x] | "sort" }
```

□

Exercise 3-5. Suppose there cannot be more than 25 stars in a line. By setting max to 25, the following program leaves the data unchanged if the longest line would fit, and otherwise scales the lines so the longest is 25 long. The new array y is used to hold the scaled lengths so that the x counts are still correct.

```
        { x[int($1/10)]++ }
END { max = MAXSTARS = 25
      for (i = 0; i <= 10; i++)
          if (x[i] > max)
              max = x[i]
      for (i = 0; i <= 10; i++)
          y[i] = x[i]/max * MAXSTARS
      for (i = 0; i < 10; i++)
          printf(" %2d - %2d: %3d %s\n",
              10*i, 10*i+9, x[i], rep(y[i],"*"))
      printf("100:      %3d %s\n", x[10], rep(y[10],"*"))
      }

function rep(n,s,  t) {  # return string of n s's
    while (n-- > 0)
        t = t s
    return t
}
```

□

Exercise 3-6. This requires two passes over the data, one to determine the range of the buckets and one to assign items to them. □

Exercise 3-7. The problem of where commas go in numbers is not clearly defined. Despite the canons of software engineering, it is common to have to solve a problem without knowing exactly what it is. Here are two possible answers. The following program sums integers that have commas in the conventional places:

```
/^[+-]?[0-9][0-9]?[0-9]?(,[0-9][0-9][0-9])*$/ {
        gsub(/,/, "")
        sum += $0
        next
}
        { print "bad format:", $0 }
END     { print sum }
```

Decimal numbers usually don't have commas after the decimal point. The program

```
/^[+-]?[0-9][0-9]?[0-9]?(,[0-9][0-9][0-9])*([.][0-9]*)?$/ {
        gsub(/,/, "")
        sum += $0
        next
}
        { print "bad format:", $0}
END     { print sum }
```

sums decimal numbers that have commas and a digit before the decimal point. □

Exercise 3-8. The function daynum(y,m,d) returns the number of days, counting from January 1, 1901. Dates are written as *year month day*, e.g., 2001 4 1. February has 29 days in years divisible by 4, except that it has 28 days in years divisible by 100 but not by 400. Thus, 1900 and 2100 are not leap years, but 2000 is.

```
function daynum(y, m, d,    days, i, n) {   # 1 == Jan 1, 1901
        split("31 28 31 30 31 30 31 31 30 31 30 31", days)
        # 365 days a year, plus one for each leap year
        n = (y-1901) * 365 + int((y-1901)/4)
        if (y % 4 == 0) # leap year from 1901 to 2099
                days[2]++
        for (i = 1; i < m; i++)
                n += days[i]
        return n + d
}
        { print daynum($1, $2, $3) }
```

This program is correct only between 1901 and 2099; it does not check the validity of its input. □

Exercise 3-11. One way to modify numtowords is as follows:

```
function numtowords(n,    cents, dols, s) { # n has 2 decimal places
        cents = substr(n, length(n)-1, 2)
        dols = substr(n, 1, length(n)-3)
        if (dols == 0)
                s = "zero dollars and " cents " cents exactly"
        else
                s = intowords(dols) " dollars and " cents " cents exactly"
        sub(/^one dollars/, "one dollar", s)
        gsub(/ +/, " ", s)
        return s
}
```

The sub command fixes "one dollars," and the gsub removes multiple blanks, even if nothing is wrong. This is easier than testing whether any changes are needed. □

Exercise 3-13. For simplicity, suppose the pairs are aa and bb, cc and dd, ee, and ff. As in the text, assume that none of these are allowed to nest or overlap.

```
BEGIN {
    expects["aa"] = "bb"
    expects["cc"] = "dd"
    expects["ee"] = "ff"
}
/^(aa|cc|ee)/ {
    if (p != "")
        print "line", NR, ": expected " p
    p = expects[substr($0, 1, 2)]
}
/^(bb|dd|ff)/ {
    x = substr($0, 1, 2)
    if (p != x) {
        print "line", NR, ": saw " x
        if (p)
            print ", expected", p
    }
    p = ""
}
END {
    if (p != "")
        print "at end, missing", p
}
```

The variable p encodes the state by recording what matching delimiter is expected. The program takes advantage of the fact that all the opening delimiters are the same length. An alternative would be to require that the delimiters always be $1. □

Exercise 3-14. Choose some marker, for instance =, that cannot be a legal pattern. Then

```
BEGIN { FS = "\t" }
/^=/   { print substr($0, 2); next }
{ printf("%s {\n\tprintf(\"line %%d, %s: %%s\\n\",NR,$0) }\n",
    $1, $2)
}
```

prints the rest of lines that start with the marker. □

Exercise 4-1. One possibility is to give the date explicitly on the command line:

```
awk -f prep3 pass=1 countries pass=2 countries |
    awk -f form3 date='January 1, 1988'
```

The variable date is then set on the command line, and its assignment can be left out of the BEGIN action of form3. As usual, some sort of quoting is needed for command-line arguments containing blanks. Another possibility is to pipe the output of the date command into the variable, as suggested in Section 3.1. □

Exercise 4-3. Before looking at our solution, check to see what yours does on numbers without decimal points. For brevity our solution just does a single column. We replace nwid by two numbers, lwid and rwid. lwid accumulates the length of the number to the left of the decimal point, and rwid counts the number of digits to the right of the decimal point and the decimal point itself. These are computed using the patterns left and right. The space needed for numbers is then lwid+rwid, which may be bigger than the length of the longest number, so the calculation for wid takes this into account.

```
# table1 - single column formatter
#    input:  one column of strings and decimal numbers
#    output: aligned column

BEGIN {
    blanks = sprintf("%100s", " ")
    number = "^[+-]?([0-9]+[.]?[0-9]*![.][0-9]+)$"
    left = "^[+-]?[0-9]*"
    right = "[.][0-9]*"
}

{   row[NR] = $1
    if ($1 ~ number) {
        match($1, left) # matches the empty string, so RLENGTH>=0
        lwid = max(lwid, RLENGTH)
        if (!match($1, right))
            RLENGTH = 0
        rwid = max(rwid, RLENGTH)
        wid = max(wid, lwid + rwid)
    } else
        wid = max(wid, length($1))
}

END {
    for (r = 1; r <= NR; r++) {
        if (row[r] ~ number)
            printf("%" wid "s\n", numjust(row[r]))
        else
            printf("%-" wid "s\n", row[r])
    }
}

function max(x, y) { return (x > y) ? x : y }

function numjust(s) {    # position s
    if (!match(s, right))
        RLENGTH = 0
    return s substr(blanks, 1, int(rwid-RLENGTH+(wid-(lwid+rwid))/2))
}
```

Each number that doesn't use all of lwid has to be shifted left, so there is a slightly more elaborate calculation in numjust. □

Exercise 4-5.

```
awk '
BEGIN { FS = "\t"; pat = ARGV[1]; ARGV[1] = "-" }
$1 ~ pat {
    printf("%s:\n", $1)
    printf("\t%d million people\n", $3)
    printf("\t%.3f million sq. mi.\n", $2/1000)
    printf("\t%.1f people per sq. mi.\n", 1000*$3/$2)
}
' "$1" <countries
```

is one way.

Another, using *var=text* on the command line instead of ARGV, is

```
awk '
BEGIN { FS = "\t" }
$1 ~ pat {
    printf("%s:\n", $1)
    printf("\t%d million people\n", $3)
    printf("\t%.3f million sq. mi.\n", $2/1000)
    printf("\t%.1f people per sq. mi.\n", 1000*$3/$2)
}
' pat="$1" <countries
```

□

Exercise 4-6. To check that the files are sorted, keep track of the last record read from each input, and compare it with the result of `getline` in `getone`. □

Exercise 4-10. Replace the loop in `doquery` that calls `system` with one that concatenates all the commands into one string `x`, for instance

```
for (j = 1; j <= ncmd[i]; j++) x = x cmd[i, j] "\n"
```

and then use `x` in the call to `system`. If `x` is made a local variable in `doquery`, it will be properly initialized on each call. □

Exercise 4-11. Here is a partial solution that remembers which derived files have been computed during one execution of `qawk`, and avoids recomputing them.

```
function doquery(s,    i,j,x) {
    for (i in qattr)  # clean up for next query
        delete qattr[i]
    query = s      # put $names in query into qattr, without $
    while (match(s, /\$[A-Za-z]+/)) {
        qattr[substr(s, RSTART+1, RLENGTH-1)] = 1
        s = substr(s, RSTART+RLENGTH+1)
    }
    for (i = 1; i <= nrel && !subset(qattr, attr, i); )
        i++
    if (i > nrel)     # didn't find a table with all attributes
        missing(qattr)
    else {            # table i contains attributes in query
        for (j in qattr)    # create awk program
            gsub("\\$" j, "$" attr[i,j], query)
        if (!exists[i] && ncmd[i] > 0) {
            for (j = 1; j <= ncmd[i]; j++)
                x = x cmd[i, j] "\n"
            print "executing\n" x  # for debugging
            if (system(x) != 0) { # create table i
                    print "command failed, query skipped\n", x
                    return
            }
            exists[i]++
        }
        awkcmd = sprintf("awk -F'\t' '%s' %s", query, relname[i])
        printf("query: %s\n", awkcmd)   # for debugging
        system(awkcmd)
    }
}
```

The array `exists` remembers which derived files have been computed. This version of `doquery` also includes the answer to the last problem. □

Exercise 4-12. The simplest answer is to change `qawk` to begin

```
BEGIN { readrel("relfile"); RS = "" }
```

Then a query consists of everything up to a blank line. Regardless of the mechanism, queries have to turn into legal awk programs. □

Exercise 5-1. The "random" numbers are of course completely deterministic: knowing the seed and the algorithm fixes the sequence of values. There are many properties, however, that the sequence shares with a random sequence. A complete discussion may be found in Knuth's *The Art of Computer Programming*, Volume 2. □

Exercise 5-2. This code generates a random set of *k* distinct integers between 1 and *n*; it is due to R. W. Floyd:

```
# print k distinct random integers between 1 and n

{ random($1, $2) }

function random(k, n,   A, i, r) {
    for (i = n-k+1; i <= n; i++)
        ((r = randint(i)) in A) ? A[i] : A[r]
    for (i in A)
        print i
}

function randint(n) { return int(n*rand())+1 }
```

□

Exercise 5-3. The problem is to generate random bridge hands of the form:

```
                            NORTH
                       S: 10 9 6 4
                       H: 8 7
                       D: J 10 6
                       C: 10 8 5 3
        WEST                                        EAST
   S: K 8 7 3                                   S: A J 5
   H: K Q 4 3 2                                 H: J
   D: 8 7                                       D: A K Q 9 2
   C: A J                                       C: K Q 6 2
                            SOUTH
                       S: Q 2
                       H: A 10 9 6 5
                       D: 5 4 3
                       C: 9 7 4
```

The program below generates a random permutation of the integers 1 through 52, which is put into the array deck. The array is sorted into four sequences of thirteen integers each. Each sequence represents a bridge hand; the integer 52 corresponds to the ace of spades, 51 to the king of spades, 1 to the deuce of clubs.

The function permute(k,n) uses Floyd's technique from the previous exercise to generate a random permutation of length k of integers between 1 and n. The function sort(x,y) uses a method called insertion sort, discussed in Section 7.1, to sort the elements in deck[x..y]. Finally, the function prhands formats and prints the four hands in the manner shown above.

```
# bridge - generate random bridge hands

BEGIN { split(permute(52,52), deck)              # generate a random deck
        sort(1,13); sort(14,26); sort(27,39); sort(40,52) # sort hands
        prhands()                                # format and print the four hands
}

function permute(k, n,     i, p, r) {    # generate a random permutation
    srand(); p = " "                     # of k integers between 1 and n
    for (i = n-k+1; i <= n; i++)
        if (p ~ " " (r = int(i*rand())+1) " " )
            sub(" " r " ", " " r " " i " ", p)     # put i after r in p
        else p = " " r p                          # put r at beginning of p
    return p
}

function sort(left,right,     i,j,t) { # sort hand in deck[left..right]
    for (i = left+1; i <= right; i++)
        for (j = i; j > left && deck[j-1] < deck[j]; j--) {
            t = deck[j-1]; deck[j-1] = deck[j]; deck[j] = t
        }
}

function prhands() {                               # print the four hands
    b = sprintf("%20s", " "); b40 = sprintf("%40s", " ")
    card = 1                              # global index into deck
    suits(13); print b "   NORTH"
    print b spds; print b hrts; print b dnds; print b clbs
    suits(26)  # create the west hand from deck[14..26]
    ws = spds substr(b40, 1, 40 - length(spds))
    wh = hrts substr(b40, 1, 40 - length(hrts))
    wd = dnds substr(b40, 1, 40 - length(dnds))
    wc = clbs substr(b40, 1, 40 - length(clbs))
    suits(39); print "   WEST" sprintf("%36s", " ") "EAST"
    print ws spds; print wh hrts; print wd dnds; print wc clbs
    suits(52); print b "   SOUTH"
    print b spds; print b hrts; print b dnds; print b clbs
}

function suits(j) {                  # collect suits of hand in deck[j-12..j]
    for (spds = "S:"; deck[card] > 39 && card <= j; card++)
        spds = spds " " fvcard(deck[card])
    for (hrts = "H:"; deck[card] > 26 && card <= j; card++)
        hrts = hrts " " fvcard(deck[card])
    for (dnds = "D:"; deck[card] > 13 && card <= j; card++)
        dnds = dnds " " fvcard(deck[card])
    for (clbs = "C:"; card <= j; card++)
        clbs = clbs " " fvcard(deck[card])
}

function fvcard(i) {                            # compute face value of card i
    if (i % 13 == 0) return "A"
    else if (i % 13 == 12) return "K"
    else if (i % 13 == 11) return "Q"
    else if (i % 13 == 10) return "J"
    else return (i % 13) + 1
}
```

□

Exercise 5-5. Doing an intelligent job on this is hard. Simplest is to keep track of how many characters have been put out, and to stop with an error message, when there are too many. Slightly more complex would be to try, in gen, only to derive the empty string or terminals, once the derivation becomes too long. Unfortunately, this won't work on every grammar every time. One guaranteed method requires knowing the shortest output each nonterminal can produce, and forcing that when the derivation becomes too long. This requires substantial processing of the grammar, and some specialized knowledge. □

Exercise 5-6. We add a probability to the end of each production. These probabilities are first read into the array rhsprob. After the grammar has been read, rhsprob is changed so that it represents the probability of this or any previous production, rather than this production. This makes the test in gen a little simpler; otherwise the probabilities would have to be be summed over and over again.

```
# sentgen1 - random sentence generator with probabilities
#    input:  grammar file; sequence of nonterminals
#    output: random sentences generated by the grammar

BEGIN {  # read rules from grammar file
    while (getline < "test-gram" > 0)
        if ($2 == "->") {
            i = ++lhs[$1]                     # count lhs
            rhsprob[$1, i] = $NF              # 0 <= probability <= 1
            rhscnt[$1, i] = NF-3             # how many in rhs
            for (j = 3; j < NF; j++)          # record them
                rhslist[$1, i, j-2] = $j
        } else
            print "illegal production: " $0
    for (sym in lhs)
        for (i = 2; i <= lhs[sym]; i++)
            rhsprob[sym, i] += rhsprob[sym, i-1]
}

{   if ($1 in lhs) {    # nonterminal to expand
        gen($1)
        printf("\n")
    } else
        print "unknown nonterminal: " $0
}

function gen(sym,    i, j) {
    if (sym in lhs) {           # a nonterminal
        j = rand()              # random production
        for (i = 1; i <= lhs[sym] && j > rhsprob[sym, i]; i++)
            ;
        for (j = 1; j <= rhscnt[sym, i]; j++) # expand rhs's
            gen(rhslist[sym, i, j])
    } else
        printf("%s ", sym)
}
```

□

Exercise 5-7. The standard approach is to replace recursion by a stack managed by the user. When expanding the right-hand side of a production, the code puts it on the stack backwards, so the output comes out in the right order.

```
# sentgen2 - random sentence generator (nonrecursive)
#   input:  grammar file; sequence of nonterminals
#   output: random sentences generated by the grammar

BEGIN {  # read rules from grammar file
    while (getline < "grammar" > 0)
        if ($2 == "->") {
            i = ++lhs[$1]                  # count lhs
            rhscnt[$1, i] = NF-2           # how many in rhs
            for (j = 3; j <= NF; j++)  # record them
                rhslist[$1, i, j-2] = $j
        } else
            print "illegal production: " $0
}

{   if ($1 in lhs) {   # nonterminal to expand
        push($1)
        gen()
        printf("\n")
    } else
        print "unknown nonterminal: " $0
}

function gen(    i, j) {
    while (stp >= 1) {
        sym = pop()
        if (sym in lhs) {          # a nonterminal
            i = int(lhs[sym] * rand()) + 1    # random production
            for (j = rhscnt[sym, i]; j >= 1; j--) # expand rhs's
                push(rhslist[sym, i, j])
        } else
            printf("%s ", sym)
    }
}

function push(s) { stack[++stp] = s }

function pop() { return stack[stp--] }
```

□

Exercise 5-9. The easiest solution is to create an initial random permutation of the integers from 1 to nq, then ask the questions in that order. □

Exercise 5-10. The cleanest way to do case conversion in awk is with an array that maps each letter; this is pretty clumsy, however, so if you have a choice it's better to use a program like the Unix command tr. □

Exercise 5-13. We accumulate the words into an array. If there are cnt words to be printed on a line, then there are cnt-1 holes to fill with spaces. If there are *n* spaces needed, each hole should have an average of *n*/(cnt-1) spaces. For each word, the program computes this number, then decrements the number of holes and spaces. If the extra blanks do not distribute evenly, the surplus ones are spread alternately from the left and from the right on successive lines, to avoid "rivers" of white space.

```
# fmt.just - formatter with right justification

BEGIN { blanks = sprintf("%60s", " ") }
/./   { for (i = 1; i <= NF; i++) addword($i) }
/^$/  { printline("no"); print "" }
END   { printline("no") }

function addword(w) {
    if (cnt + size + length(w) > 60)
        printline("yes")
    line[++cnt] = w
    size += length(w)
}

function printline(f,     i, nb, nsp, holes) {
    if (f == "no" || cnt == 1) {
        for (i = 1; i <= cnt; i++)
            printf("%s%s", line[i], i < cnt ? " " : "\n")
    } else if (cnt > 1) {
        dir = 1 - dir          # alternate side for extra blanks
        nb = 60 - size         # number of blanks needed
        holes = cnt - 1        # holes
        for (i = 1; holes > 0; i++) {
            nsp = int((nb-dir) / holes) + dir
            printf("%s%s", line[i], substr(blanks, 1, nsp))
            nb -= nsp
            holes--
        }
        print line[cnt]
    }
    size = cnt = 0
}
```

A "no" argument to `printline` avoids right-justifying the last line of a paragraph. □

Exercise 5-15. It depends on whether the defective name appears anywhere else in the document. If it does, it will be erroneously substituted away. □

Exercise 5-16.
```
/^\.#/ { printf("{ gsub(/%s/, \"%d\") }\n", $2, ++count[$1])
         if (saw[$2])
             print NR ": redefinition of", $2, "from line", saw[$2]
         saw[$2] = NR
       }
END    { printf("!/^[.]#/\n") }
```
□

Exercise 5-18.
```
/^\.#/ { s[$2] = ++count[$1]; next }
       { for (i in s)
             gsub(i, s[i])
         print
       }
```
The definition of a symbolic name must come before it is used. □

Exercise 5-19. The easiest solution consonant with the divide-and-conquer strategy is to add a filter to the pipeline to delete rotated lines that begin with a word from the stop list:

```
    ...
    awk '$1 !~ /^(a|an|and|by|for|if|in|is|of|on|the|to)$/' |
    sort -f |
    ...
```

☐

Exercise 5-23. How to distinguish between a literal ~ and the ~ used as a space is a question of style. We will use the awk escape sequence convention: \ before the character when we want the literal character. We'll consider only ~; the others are just elaborations in both `ix.genkey` and `ix.format`. For ~, we replace all instances of \~ by some string that cannot occur, namely a tab followed by 1. No string containing a tab can occur, because tab is the field separator. The remaining tildes are substituted away, and the escaped ones are put back, unescaped. Thus, the first gsub in `ix.genkey` is replaced by

```
    gsub(/\~/, "\t1", $1)    # protect quoted tildes
    gsub(/~/, " ", $1)       # unprotected tildes now become blanks
    gsub(/\t1/, "~", $1)     # restore protected tildes
```

Also, the tildes should no longer be removed from the sort key. ☐

Exercise 6-1. Only four lines have to be added, two in pass 1 and two in pass 2.

```
    ...
    # ASSEMBLER PASS 1
        nextmem = 0      # new
        FS = "[ \t]+"
        while (getline <srcfile > 0) {
            input[nextmem] = $0    # new: remember source line
            sub(/#.*/, "")         # strip comments
            symtab[$1] = nextmem   # remember label location
            if ($2 != "") {        # save op, addr if present
                print $2 "\t" $3 >tempfile
                nextmem++
            }
        }
        close(tempfile)

    # ASSEMBLER PASS 2
        nextmem = 0
        while (getline <tempfile > 0) {
            if ($2 !~ /^[0-9]*$/)  # if symbolic addr,
                $2 = symtab[$2]    # replace by numeric value
            mem[nextmem++] = 1000 * op[$1] + $2  # pack into word
        }
        for (i = 0; i < nextmem; i++)    # new: print memory
            printf("%3d:  %05d   %s\n", i, mem[i], input[i])  # new
    }
    ...
```

☐

Exercise 6-6. It's surprisingly difficult to find some simple modification of graph to do this, because knowledge of x and y is embedded throughout the program, and in many variables like bticks and lticks. Perhaps more fruitful is to define a filter transpose that processes the input. Here is one, obtained by editing graph to take the appropriate action for each kind of line.

```
# transpose - input and output suitable for graph
#    input:  data and specification of a graph
#    output: data and specification for the transposed graph

BEGIN {
    number = "^[-+]?([0-9]+[.]?[0-9]*|[.][0-9]+)" \
                         "([eE][-+]?[0-9]+)?$"
}
$1 == "bottom" && $2 == "ticks" {      # ticks for x-axis
    $1 = "left"
    print
    next
}
$1 == "left" && $2 == "ticks" {        # ticks for y-axis
    $1 = "bottom"
    print
    next
}
$1 == "range" {                        # xmin ymin xmax ymax
    print $1, $3, $2, $5, $4
    next
}
$1 == "height" { $1 = "width"; print; next }
$1 == "width"  { $1 = "height"; print; next }
$1 ~ number && $2 ~ number   { nd++; print $2, $1, $3; next }
$1 ~ number && $2 !~ number { # single number:
    nd++                       #    count data points
    print $1, nd, $2           #    fill in both x and y
    next
}
{ print }
```

A simple version of logarithmic axes could be done the same way. □

Exercise 6-13. These are all just additional cases in the large if statement. For instance,

```
else if ($i == "pi")
    stack[++top] = 3.14159265358979
```

□

Exercise 7-1. The condition A[i] > A[i+1] is essentially the invariant that is enforced by the algorithm, so it should be true automatically. The real problem is that check doesn't check that the output is a permutation of the input: it won't notice if elements are moved outside of the proper array bounds. □

Exercise 7-3. As described briefly in Chapter 8, awk uses a hash table to store arrays. These hash tables allow constant-time lookup of elements in small arrays, but take more time as the arrays grow. □

Exercise 7-8. The END action inserted by makeprof is executed after any other END's that might be present, so an exit in an earlier END would stop the program. A partial fix is to change makeprof to print its END action before anything else. □

Exercise 7-10. Again, push the nodes onto a stack instead of printing them, then print the stack from the bottom after the end of the input. Alternatively, reverse the roles of $1 and $2, either in rtsort or by a separate program. □